W9-CPG-883

THREATS TO CIVIL LIBERTIES

Threats to Civil Liberties:
VOTING

Stuart A. Kallen

ReferencePoint
Press®

San Diego, CA

About the Author

Stuart A. Kallen is the author of more than 350 nonfiction books for children and young adults. He has written on topics ranging from the theory of relativity to the art of electronic dance music. In addition, Kallen has written award-winning children's videos and television scripts. In his spare time he is a singer, songwriter, and guitarist in San Diego.

© 2019 ReferencePoint Press, Inc.
Printed in the United States

For more information, contact:
ReferencePoint Press, Inc.
PO Box 27779
San Diego, CA 92198
www.ReferencePointPress.com

ALL RIGHTS RESERVED.
No part of this work covered by the copyright hereon may be reproduced or used in any form or by any means—graphic, electronic, or mechanical, including photocopying, recording, taping, web distribution, or information storage retrieval systems—without the written permission of the publisher.

LIBRARY OF CONGRESS CATALOGING-IN-PUBLICATION DATA

Name: Kallen, Stuart A., author.
Title: Threats to Civil Liberties: Voting/by Stuart A. Kallen.
Description: San Diego, CA: ReferencePoint Press, Inc., [2019] | Series:
Threats to Civil Liberties | Includes bibliographical references and index.
Identifiers:| ISBN 9781682824580 (eBook) | ISBN 9781682824573
(hardback)
Subjects: LCSH: Voting—United States—Juvenile literature.| Civil
rights—United States—Juvenile literature.

CONTENTS

R0453873074

Voting Rights Restrictions

The US Constitution guarantees rights that Americans have fiercely defended for more than two centuries. For example, most Americans would never accept restrictions on free speech, free assembly, or freedom of religion. Occasionally, though, the extent of these rights has been tested and debated in court. The right to vote is among those civil rights that has undergone legal scrutiny. Politicians and judges have repeatedly sought limits on voting rights despite the fact that the Fifteenth Amendment to the Constitution declares that "the right of citizens of the United States to vote shall not be denied or abridged by the United States or by any State on account of race, color, or previous condition of servitude." These rights have been challenged—and sometimes jeopardized—whenever the political status quo was threatened by marginalized voters seeking equal representation.

One Million Prevented from Voting

The Fifteenth Amendment was added to the Constitution in 1870, five years after the Civil War put an end to slavery. The phrase "previous condition of servitude" referred to freed African American men who were granted the right to vote by the amendment. The Constitution was amended again in 1920, when the Nineteenth Amendment granted women the right to vote. But in recent years hundreds of state laws have been passed that have had the effect of abridging, or imposing restrictions on, voting rights. Since the right to vote in elections is called the franchise, the effect of these laws is referred to as disenfranchisement.

According to a comprehensive study by political scientist Charles Stewart of the Massachusetts Institute of Technology, an estimated 16 million people—12 percent of the American electorate—encountered at least one problem voting in the 2016 presidential election. As a result, an estimated 1 million people were prevented from exercising their right to vote. Some problems were due to bureaucratic mix-ups. However, most disenfranchisement was due to voter restrictions that reduced the number of polling places, cut early voting opportunities, and required voters to show certain forms of government-issued identification (ID) before casting a ballot.

To understand why some states make it harder for people to vote, it helps to explore some basic facts about the political parties in the United States. According to the Pew Research Center, 48 percent of all registered voters in 2016 identified as Democrats or leaned Democratic. This compares with 44 percent who identified as Republican or leaned Republican. Although voters are closely split between the two major parties, there are major differences when pollsters examine how various groups vote. For example, nearly 90 percent of African Americans and 66 percent of Latino and Asian Americans identify as Democrats. Likewise, around 55 percent of millennial voters—people under the age of thirty—vote for Democratic candidates. The numbers for Republicans are almost a mirror opposite. White males over the age of forty-five make up around 63 percent of Republican voters.

Although Democrats have an advantage among young people and minority voters, some election observers maintain that Republicans have successfully preserved their electoral advantage by passing laws to limit the franchise for Democratic voters. Since 2010 Republicans in twenty-six state legislatures have passed hundreds of laws that make it harder to vote, including strict voter ID requirements. As Dale Ho, the director of the American Civil Liberties Union (ACLU) Voting Rights Project, explains, "We see [voting] restrictions popping up like mushrooms in . . . states with large minority populations. . . . Laws that require you to have a particular ID to cast a ballot disproportionately impact . . . poorer voters who don't have the same access to documentation and IDs as the rest of us."[1] To critics like Ho, the result is the disenfranchisement of numerous voters who might tip elections.

Claims of Voting Fraud in the 2016 Presidential Election

Around half of the restrictive voting laws first went into effect before the 2016 presidential election. In the run-up to the election, Republican candidate Donald J. Trump repeated the unproven allegation that the American election system was "rigged" to favor his Democratic opponent, Hillary Clinton. As Trump stated at an August campaign rally, "The election is going to be rigged. . . . People are going to walk in and they're going to vote ten times, maybe. . . . The only way we can lose . . . is if cheating goes on."[2]

> "The election is going to be rigged. . . . People are going to walk in and they're going to vote ten times, maybe. . . . The only way we can lose . . . is if cheating goes on."[2]
>
> —Republican presidential candidate Donald J. Trump

On election day Trump claimed victory after receiving a winning margin of votes from the electoral college. However, Clinton won the popular vote by around 3 million.

Perhaps because he lost the popular vote to Clinton, Trump continued to spin stories about election fraud, arguing that 3 to 5 million people illegally voted in the 2016 election. Trump based his notion on a 2012 report by the Pew Charitable Trusts that found millions of invalid names on voter registration rolls. These included registrations for nearly 2 million people who were deceased but were still listed as voters. Additionally, around 2.7 million voters were registered in more than one state because they had moved. However, the author of the Pew report made it clear

The right to vote has undergone legal scrutiny over the years. Politicians and judges have repeatedly sought limits on voting rights for various reasons.

that invalid registrations do not correlate to illegal votes. In fact, multiple nationwide studies have uncovered only a handful of incidents where noncitizens voted or where people actually voted more than once.

A 2014 study by Loyola Law School professor Justin Levitt supported the conclusion that voter fraud is a political illusion. Levitt studied more than 1 billion ballots cast between 2000 and 2014. He found that only 31 fraudulent votes were cast at polling places. This backs assertions by state election officials in both parties who say that noncitizens rarely, if ever, vote in American elections. Although voting fraud is rare, politicians continue to justify laws that make it harder to vote for some groups. As Ho says, "The kind of fraud that these laws are supposedly enacted to prevent happens less frequently than Americans being struck by lightning."[3] However, some conservative politicians continue to claim that voter fraud is more widespread than people like Ho might believe.

Hanging onto Power

Americans do not need to present ID or meet any other conditions to practice the right of free speech or freedom of religion. However, some politicians view voting rights as a privilege to be granted to some—but not all—Americans. In the United States every citizen over the age of eighteen has the right to vote. But the integrity of the American electoral system is compromised every time an eligible voter is turned away at the polls. Those who fight for voting rights believe that politicians who favor some voters over others pose a bigger threat to democracy. As Todd Allbaugh, an aide to a Wisconsin Republican state legislator, explains, some "elected officials [are] . . . happy to help deny a fellow American's constitutional right to vote in order to increase their own chances to hang onto power."[4] As long as politicians can push election laws to work in their favor, the threat to voting rights will continue.

"The kind of fraud that these laws are supposedly enacted to prevent happens less frequently than Americans being struck by lightning."[3]

—Dale Ho, the director of the ACLU Voting Rights Project

CHAPTER 1

The Voting Rights Act

Fannie Mae Hamer was an African American farmworker who lived in the small town of Ruleville, Mississippi. In August 1962 Hamer traveled to the Sunflower County courthouse in Indianola, Mississippi, to register to vote. The county clerk presented Hamer with a registration document, officially called a literacy test, which contained twenty-one questions. Literacy tests were only given to black citizens who tried to register to vote. Some questions—such as "What is today's date?"—were simple. However, trivial errors, such as missing a comma in the date, would lead to immediate disqualification. Other questions were chilling. The county wanted the name of Hamer's employer. As Hamer explained, "This meant that you would be fired by the time you got back home [for registering to vote]."[5]

Hamer's desire to vote overcame her fear of unemployment, and she completed most of the questions on the literacy test. The county clerk then produced a copy of the Mississippi state constitution. One of the last questions on the literacy test required Hamer to write a paragraph explaining the meaning of complex regulations in the constitution called de facto laws. As Hamer later joked, "I knowed as much about de facto laws as a horse knows about Christmas Day."[6] Hamer could not provide a response that was satisfactory to the county clerk, and she was not allowed to register to vote.

The next day, for attempting to practice her constitutional right to vote, Hamer was fired from her job and evicted from the plantation where she had worked and lived for eighteen years. Undaunted, Hamer studied the state constitution and passed the literacy test in January 1963. But when she tried to vote in the primary election the following March, she could not cast a ballot. She was told she had failed to pay what was called a poll tax. The Mississippi poll tax was two dollars, equal to fifteen dollars in 2017. Hamer went home, gathered the money, paid the poll tax, and voted. Hamer went on to become one of the leading voting rights activists of the 1960s. Along the way, she was arrested, severely beaten, and shot at simply for trying to exercise her voting rights.

Violence Against Voters

Although the US Constitution guarantees the right to vote, it grants the states the power to set voting requirements. The Mississippi regulations that prevented Hamer and other African Americans from voting were common throughout the Deep South during the mid-twentieth century. Literacy tests and poll taxes were enforced in Alabama, Georgia, Louisiana, South Carolina, Virginia, and elsewhere. In some states, such as Louisiana, the literacy tests contained confusing, convoluted questions that were impossible to answer. Revered civil rights activist and Georgia congressman John Lewis describes the test administered by county clerks in his home state of Alabama:

> [The literacy test] was a sixty-eight-question survey about obscure aspects of state and federal regulation. Citizens might be asked to recite verbatim long portions of the U.S. Constitution. Some were even asked irrelevant questions such as the number of bubbles in a bar of soap. Black people with Ph.D. and M.A. degrees were routinely told they did not read well enough to pass the test.[7]

Revered civil rights activist and Georgia congressman John Lewis (pictured) advocates against the use of literacy tests as a voting requirement. He believes the tests discriminate against African Americans.

Literacy tests were quite effective. Lewis grew up in Lowness County, Alabama, where African Americans made up 80 percent of the population; despite their majority, no black person was registered to vote. In Mississippi, African Americans made up 65 percent of the population in 1960, but only 2 percent were registered to vote. Whites, who made up 33 percent of the state, held all political offices. Many police officers, sheriffs, and politicians openly supported or were members of racist organizations, including the White Citizens' Council and the Ku Klux Klan. These groups promoted violence and terror to retain political power. As Lewis writes, "People who tried to register to vote or who encouraged black citizens to register were arrested, jailed, beaten, and killed. Some were fired from their jobs, separated from their families, evicted from their homes, and threatened with the loss of everything they had."[8]

The Voting Rights Act

Lewis worked with Martin Luther King Jr. and other civil rights activists to protest voting restrictions in the South. On Sunday, March 7, 1965, Lewis attended a demonstration that attracted national attention. Around six hundred civil rights activists attempted to peacefully march from Selma, Alabama, to the state capitol in Montgomery to demand their constitutional right to vote. They were stopped by state troopers and mounted deputies in full riot gear and were ordered to disperse. When the demonstrators kneeled to pray, authorities sprayed them with tear gas. In what became known as Bloody Sunday, the activists were whipped with bullwhips, beaten with billy clubs, and trampled under the hooves of horses. Lewis suffered a fractured skull. But Bloody Sunday proved to be a turning point in the quest for voting rights. Regular television programming was interrupted across the nation that day, and millions of Americans sat in their living rooms watching shocking news footage of peaceful protesters beaten bloody.

> "People who tried to register to vote . . . were arrested, jailed, beaten, and killed. Some were fired from their jobs, separated from their families, evicted from their homes, and threatened with the loss of everything they had."[8]
>
> —US representative John Lewis of Georgia

Eight days after Bloody Sunday, President Lyndon B. Johnson called a joint session of Congress to introduce voting rights legislation. In a moving speech, Johnson called the Selma demonstration "a turning point in man's unending search for freedom."[9] Five months later, on August 6, large majorities in both houses of Congress passed the Voting Rights Act of 1965. At the signing ceremony, Johnson made clear that supporting the act was a moral duty for all Americans: "This act flows from a clear and simple wrong. Its only purpose is to right that wrong. Millions of Americans are denied the right to vote because of their color. This law will ensure them the right to vote. The wrong is one which no American, in his heart, can justify. The right is one which no American, true to our principles, can deny."[10]

The Voting Rights Act reinforces the language of the Fifteenth Amendment, which prohibits any practice that might deny or abridge the right to vote because of race. Another general provision in the law forbids the use of poll taxes and literacy tests. Anyone who attempted to interfere with the right to vote could face civil and criminal penalties.

Special Provisions

The Voting Rights Act also contains special provisions. A provision called Section 4 was written because voter discrimination was more prevalent in southern states and certain counties located in four other states. All areas covered by Section 4—states and counties—are referred to as jurisdictions. Section 4 created what is called a coverage formula, based on voting data, to determine where voter restrictions were in place as of November 1964. The jurisdictions in the coverage formula included Alabama, Alaska, Georgia, Louisiana, Mississippi, South Carolina, Texas, and Virginia. The coverage formula also singled out counties in Arizona, Hawaii, Idaho, and North Carolina where voting rights were denied to various groups, including Hispanics, Native Americans, Pacific Islanders, and African Americans.

Congress amended Section 4 of the Voting Rights Act several times after its initial passage. One significant change was enacted in 1975, when the law was expanded to cover so-called language minorities, which Congress defined as Native Americans, Asian Americans, Alaska Natives, or voters of Spanish heritage. Lawmakers felt these voters needed extra protection at a time when states like Arizona and Texas were only printing ballots in English.

During a peaceful march in Selma, Alabama, in 1965, civil rights activists were injured when state police violently broke up the demonstration. The incident became known as Bloody Sunday and became a turning point in the quest for equal voting rights.

A second provision of the Voting Rights Act, Section 5, required the covered jurisdictions to obtain federal permission before making any changes in their voting laws. Permission could be granted by the state's attorney general or by a three-judge panel on the district court in Washington, DC. Under Section 5, the jurisdictions were required to prove that proposed voting changes would not negatively impact any individual's right to vote on the basis of race or minority status.

The Section 5 process is called preclearance. Officials must preapprove, or clear, minor changes to voting procedures, like moving a polling place. Preclearance was also required for major changes, such as requiring voters to present certain types of identification. Lewis explains how Section 5 works: "The federal government essentially has the power to stop discriminatory voting changes before they are enacted into law. Therefore, Section

14

5 serves as a significant deterrent to the advancement of discriminatory legislation, making jurisdictions seriously consider the impact of changes they propose."[11]

Striking Down the Law

According to a 1965 Gallup poll, 76 percent of Americans approved of the Voting Rights Act. However, between 1966 and 2009, opponents challenged various sections of the law in court twenty-one times. The first case was decided only five months after the law was enacted. Claiming the law was a punitive and unconstitutional infringement on states' rights, South Carolina sued the government to overturn the preclearance provisions in Section 5. The state lost the case when the Supreme Court ruled that this provision was a valid way to enforce the voting rights guaranteed by the Constitution. Section 5 was upheld as constitutional by the Supreme Court two more times, in 1980 and 1999.

However, Section 5 of the Voting Rights Act was not permanent; Congress was required to renew it periodically. Lawmakers extended Section 5 in 1970, in 1975, and for twenty-five years in 1982. In 2006 Congress held hearings that highlighted the persistence of racial discrimination at polling places. Representatives voted overwhelmingly (390 to 33) to extend the preclearance requirement for another twenty-five years. However, when Section 5 was extended, Congress used the coverage formula from 1975 to determine which jurisdictions would be required to seek preclearance. After Congress passed the extension, some observers noted that the racial dynamics had substantially shifted in the South since 1975 and the coverage formula was outdated.

In 2010 officials in Shelby County, Alabama, found other problems with Sections 4 and 5 of the Voting Rights Act. Shelby County, which was 90 percent white at the time, did not want to spend time, energy, and taxpayer dollars to obtain preclearance for minor changes related to voting laws. Shelby County attorney Frank "Butch" Ellis believed the law was an expensive burden: "We [have] to go to Washington for pre-clearance just

The Voting Rights Act Is Outdated

In 2013 the Supreme Court struck down Section 4 of the Voting Rights Act, which required nine southern states, and cities and counties in seven other states, to seek federal approval before changing their voting laws. The court ruled that the provision was no longer relevant when Congress reauthorized the act in 2006. Chief Justice John Roberts wrote in the decision,

> History did not end in 1965. By the time the [Voting Rights] Act was reauthorized in 2006, there had been 40 more years of it. . . . During that time, largely because of the Voting Rights Act, voting tests were abolished, disparities in voter registration and turnout due to race were erased, and African-Americans attained political office in record numbers. And yet . . . [Congress] ignores these developments, keeping the focus on decades-old data relevant to decades-old problems, rather than current data reflecting current needs.

> The Fifteenth Amendment [to the Constitution] commands that the right to vote shall not be denied or abridged on account of race or color, and it gives Congress the power to enforce that command. The Amendment is not designed to punish [states] for the past; its purpose is to ensure a better future.

Quoted in John Schwartz, "*Shelby County v. Holder*: Between the Lines of the Voting Rights Act Opinion," *New York Times*, June 25, 2013. www.nytimes.com.

to move a polling station from one church to another church across the street."[12]

Ellis filed a lawsuit against US attorney general Eric Holder, a case referred to as *Shelby County v. Holder*. Ellis argued that Sections 4 and 5 of the Voting Rights Act were unconstitutional. He sought a permanent injunction (ban) against enforcement of the provisions. After losing in lower courts, Shelby County appealed to the Supreme Court, which agreed to hear the case. In June 2013 the Supreme Court struck down Section 4 of the Voting Rights Act

The Voting Rights Act Is Still Needed

In 2013 Section 4 of the Voting Rights Act, which required certain jurisdictions to obtain federal permission to make changes in voting laws, was struck down by the Supreme Court. President Barack Obama released the following statement:

> I am deeply disappointed with the Supreme Court's decision today. For nearly 50 years, the Voting Rights Act—enacted and repeatedly renewed by wide bipartisan majorities in Congress—has helped secure the right to vote for millions of Americans. Today's decision invalidating one of its core provisions upsets decades of well-established practices that help make sure voting is fair, especially in places where voting discrimination has been historically prevalent.

> As a nation, we've made a great deal of progress towards guaranteeing every American the right to vote. But, as the Supreme Court recognized, voting discrimination still exists. And while today's decision is a setback, it doesn't represent the end of our efforts to end voting discrimination. I am calling on Congress to pass legislation to ensure every American has equal access to the polls. My Administration will continue to do everything in its power to ensure a fair and equal voting process.

Barack Obama, "Statement by the President on the Supreme Court Ruling in *Shelby County v. Holder*," White House, June 25, 2013. https://obamawhitehouse.archives.gov.

in a 5–4 decision. Lewis reacted to the judgment: "Today the Supreme Court stuck a dagger in the heart of the Voting Rights Act of 1965. . . . History is relevant because voting rights have been given in this country, and they have been taken away."[13]

Chief justice John Roberts wrote the opinion that explained why the provision was unconstitutional. He stated that Section 4 made sense when it was enacted in 1965. But Congress was wrong to use voting data from 1975 to justify renewal of the provision in 2006 because African Americans were now serving as mayors, congressional representatives, and other elected officials.

Roberts said Congress did not use information that related to these current realities; instead, he wrote, "it re-enacted a formula based on 40-year-old facts having no logical relationship to the present day." Roberts further noted that states cannot be punished for deeds committed in the past: "Our country has changed, and while any racial discrimination in voting is too much, Congress must ensure that the legislation it passes to remedy that problem speaks to current conditions."[14]

Although Section 5 was not ruled unconstitutional, the provision is meaningless without the coverage formula provided by Section 4. Supreme Court justice Ruth Bader Ginsburg, who voted to uphold Section 4, voiced her opinion in a written dissent: "Throwing out preclearance when it has worked and is continuing to work to stop discriminatory changes is like throwing away your umbrella in a rainstorm because you are not getting wet."[15]

The effects of the Supreme Court ruling were immediate. Within hours, Texas implemented a controversial voter ID law that had been blocked as discriminatory in 2012 by the Justice Department. The Texas law required voters to present a driver's license, passport, military ID, or concealed-gun permit. In what critics viewed as a move to reduce the franchise for young people, student ID cards were not accepted. According to voting advocacy group the Brennan Center for Justice, more than six hundred thousand Texas voters lacked the identification needed to vote. Most of them were black, Hispanic, young, or elderly.

> "Our country has changed, and while any racial discrimination in voting is too much, Congress must ensure that the legislation it passes to remedy that problem speaks to current conditions."[14]
>
> —John Roberts, chief justice of the United States

In 2013, the US Supreme Court struck down Section 4 of the Voting Rights Act in a 5–4 decision. Justice Ruth Bader Ginsburg (pictured), a civil rights advocate, voted to uphold Section 4.

Failing to Fix the Voting Rights Act

When Roberts helped strike down Section 4 of the Voting Rights Act, he noted that Congress was free to pass a bill that contained updated voting data. Congress made several attempts to do so. In 2014 the Voting Rights Amendment Act was proposed, which would have created a new coverage formula. The act would have required preclearance in states that had passed voting laws that violated federal law five times during the previous fifteen years. At the time, this would have covered Georgia, Louisiana, Texas, and Mississippi. Local jurisdictions would have been included if they committed three or more voting rights violations. The bill, however, failed to attract enough Republican votes in Congress to pass.

On the fiftieth anniversary of the Voting Rights Act, a second bill, the Voting Rights Advancement Act of 2015, was introduced in Congress. The act would have allowed the attorney general to place federal observers at the polls to ensure everyone's right to vote. This act also would have established a new formula to decide which states would need government permission to change voting laws. The Advancement Act was sponsored by Lewis, who stated, "It's important to fix a decision of the United States Supreme Court and make it easier, make it simple for all of our people to participate in a democratic process. . . . It is a bill for the next generation, and helps protect the legacy of the previous generation who fought so hard five decades ago for these voting rights protections."[16]

Despite the impassioned words, Republicans controlled Congress in 2015, and few believed the new legislation was necessary. Bob Goodlatte, the chairman of the House Judiciary Committee, stated, "We are certainly willing to look at any new evidence of discrimination if there is a need to take any measures. But at this point in time, we have not seen that, and therefore no changes [are needed]."[17] Goodlatte's argument—like the arguments of other conservative critics—rested on the idea that voting discrimination was a relic of the past, not a current concern. Without Goodlatte's support, the Voting Rights Advancement Act of 2015 was never put up for a vote in the House of Representatives.

> "We are certainly willing to look at any new evidence of discrimination if there is a need to take any measures. But at this point in time, we have not seen that."[17]
>
> —US representative Bob Goodlatte of Virginia

The Cost of Confusion

By 2015 eight of the nine states previously requiring preclearance passed new voting laws. Many of the laws, including those in Texas, were challenged in court. Without preclearance, however, those who file lawsuits, called plaintiffs, cannot stop an offending law until after it goes into effect. Plaintiffs are also required to show that the discrimination personally harmed them, which is much more difficult to prove in court. Additionally, plaintiffs must pay for lawyers while covering other legal expenses, and the disenfranchised are often poorer minorities who do not have the means.

Despite the difficulties, some of the new voter restrictions were struck down. But laws in Texas and other states remained in place during the 2014 elections. Although these states were eventually required to loosen voter restrictions, there was another negative effect. The confusion over ID requirements and other voting changes dampened turnout. As Lloyd Leonard of the League of Women Voters said in 2016, "One of the greatest impediments to voting is confusion. In some pretty important states the rules are still changing."[18] Though much has changed since Fannie Lou Hamer tried to register in 1962, voting rights are still being contested. As long as politicians see an advantage to placing obstacles in front of some voters, the battle over voting rights will continue in street protests and in federal courtrooms.

> "One of the greatest impediments to voting is confusion. In some pretty important states the rules are still changing."[18]
>
> —Lloyd Leonard, Senior Director for Advocacy, League of Women Voters

CHAPTER 2

Voter IDs and Early Voting

In 2010 Republican activists were angry at President Barack Obama and the Democrats who controlled Congress. Republicans were united in their opposition to the health care program known as the Affordable Care Act (ACA). Although the ACA aimed to help millions of previously uninsured Americans obtain medical insurance, Republicans did not believe that the government should have the power to regulate the health care industry. They derisively called the act Obamacare.

Democrats had controlled the House and the Senate since 2008, when Obama was elected. But in November 2010 Democrats suffered a massive defeat at the polls. In one of the largest victories for a political party in nearly a century, Republicans gained 63 seats in the House of Representatives and 6 Senate seats. The results were equally dramatic in state elections, where Republicans gained 680 seats in statehouses across the country. Before the election, Democrats controlled twenty-seven state legislatures and Republicans were in charge of fourteen (eight states were split between the parties). After the election, those numbers nearly flipped, with Republicans taking control of twenty-six state legislatures.

Almost immediately after the upset, victorious Republican legislatures across the country introduced bills that changed long-standing voting procedures. The bills limited early voting hours, mandated certain forms of identification, and even required voters to prove they were US citizens. Not all of the bills passed, but twenty-two states had new restrictions on voting by the time the 2014 elections were held. According to the Brennan Center for Justice, these bills affected more than 5 million voters nationwide.

Singling Out Minority and College Voters

Some of the most dramatic voter rights challenges took place in Wisconsin, where a Republican majority took control of the state legislature in January 2011. According to the Wisconsin Legislative Council, Republican governor Scott Walker signed thirty-three pieces of legislation that affected how residents could vote. Act 23—one of the bills signed by Walker in May 2011—was considered among the harshest voter ID laws in the nation. Wisconsin citizens who wanted to vote would be required to produce a few specific forms of identification that not all citizens possessed. Permitted IDs included a driver's license, passport, military ID card, college photo ID, or one of several other—fairly uncommon—documents.

Wisconsin Republicans argued that Act 23 was needed to fight widespread voter fraud. Supporters of the act often cite a 2008 Supreme Court ruling that upheld Indiana's voter ID law. In that ruling, Justice John Paul Stevens asserted,

> It remains true . . . that flagrant examples of such fraud in other parts of the country have been documented throughout this nation's history by respected historians and journalists, that occasional examples have surfaced in recent years, and that Indiana's own experience with fraudulent voting . . . demonstrate that not only is the risk of voter fraud real but that it could affect the outcome of a close election.[19]

However, critics maintained that voter fraud was not a problem in Wisconsin according to Dale Schultz, a Republican legislator first elected in 1983. In 2011 Schultz ordered his staff to

A young woman shows identification to vote at a local polling station. In order to prevent voter fraud, Wisconsin passed laws in 2011 requiring multiple forms of identification to vote. These laws made it more difficult for some legitimate voters to vote.

launch an investigation to find three concrete examples of voter fraud. As Schultz stated in a 2017 interview, "They couldn't do it. . . . [They] made it clear that there was no voter fraud happening."[20] Schultz was dismayed by his party's focus on voter fraud and chose not to run for reelection in 2014.

Some observers argued that Act 23 made it harder for some Wisconsin voters to cast a ballot. A study by the voter rights group One Wisconsin showed that three hundred thousand registered voters in the state did not possess the types of ID required by Act 23, equal to 9 percent of all state voters. Those without proper IDs could obtain a state identification card at the Wisconsin Department of Motor Vehicles (DMV). Yet several months after Walker signed Act 23, his administration announced plans to close numerous DMV offices, ostensibly as a cost-cutting measure. Opponents claimed the proposed closures were in districts that were largely Democratic. Public outcry forced Walker to keep all existing DMV offices open, but other obstacles remained.

To obtain a state ID, Wisconsin citizens are required to produce one or more documents to prove their identity. Required credentials might include out-of-state photo IDs, birth certificates, and marriage certificates. Numerous academic studies show that these requirements deprive voting rights to low-income citizens, minorities, the young, the elderly, and people with disabilities. The most common form of ID is a driver's license, but millions of minorities do not drive because they cannot afford cars or do not require them because they live in urban areas where public transit is available. According a 2012 study cited by former attorney general Eric Holder, 25 percent of voting-age African Americans in the United States lack a driver's license compared to 8 percent for whites.

There are other problems for those who try to obtain the proper identification to cast a ballot. The proper paperwork to get an official ID costs money and requires citizens to take time to travel to the DMV or other government offices. According to the ACLU, the combined cost to obtain a government-issued ID ranges from $75 to $175 for document fees, travel expenses, and missed work. These requirements can hamper poor voters from securing a proper ID.

The Difficulties of Setting Records Straight

Some voters who spend the time and money are still denied IDs. The case of seventy-four-year-old Johnny Randle, an African American resident of Wisconsin, exemplifies the problem. Randle moved from Mississippi to Milwaukee in 2011, after Act 23 went into effect. In order to obtain a Wisconsin ID, Randle was required to present his Mississippi birth certificate at the Milwaukee DMV. But Randle had never had a copy of the document, which had been issued in 1937.

Randle's daughter paid the state of Mississippi twenty-four dollars to get a copy of her father's birth certificate. When the document arrived, the name listed, Johnnie Marton Randall, did not match the spelling that Johnny Martin Randle had used his entire life. A DMV worker told Randle he would have to either correct his name through the Social Security Administration (SSA) or go to court to legally change the name he used his entire life to match the name on his birth certificate. Randle, who survived on disability payments from the SSA, was afraid that changing his name with the agency might interrupt the monthly payments he depended on. The cost of legally changing his name was time-consuming and cost more than Randle could afford. When the April 5, 2012, presidential primary election was held in Wisconsin, Randle could not vote for his favored candidate, Barack Obama. During the 1960s Randle had fought for his voting rights in Mississippi. In 2012 he was disenfranchised in Wisconsin.

The case of Christine Krucki exemplifies how voter ID laws can affect the elderly. Krucki was born in 1925 in the small town of Lublin, Wisconsin, and had voted in every election since 1948. In 2012, when attempting to get a Wisconsin state ID, Krucki discovered that her maiden name as written on her birth certificate did not match the name on her marriage certificate. Krucki learned that it would cost around $200 to amend the marriage certificate. In 2013 Krucki enlisted the help of her daughter, Sharon Erickson, to obtain a state-issued ID, but her efforts failed. Erickson wrote an angry letter to Governor Walker telling her mother's story: "We want you to know how the law that you supported and signed into law affects your constituency in an extremely negative way. Why are the Wisconsin Republicans as well as the Republicans nationwide attempting to rig elections by stifling the right to vote of good and honest Americans?"[21]

> "Why are the Wisconsin Republicans as well as the Republicans nationwide attempting to rig elections by stifling the right to vote of good and honest Americans?"[21]
>
> —Sharon Erickson, a Wisconsin voter

In 2013 Randle and Krucki were both parties in a lawsuit that challenged Act 23. Like many lawsuits that seek to overturn voter ID laws, the lawsuit took a long, circuitous path through the

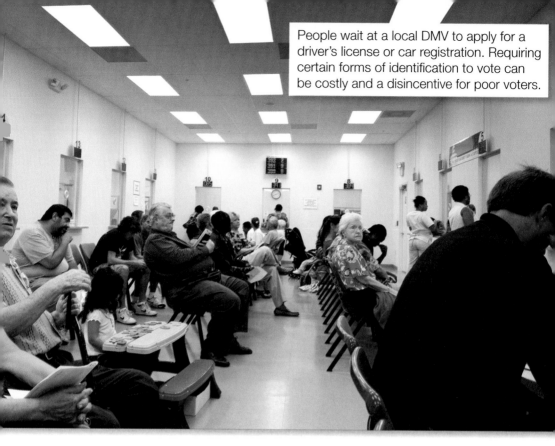

People wait at a local DMV to apply for a driver's license or car registration. Requiring certain forms of identification to vote can be costly and a disincentive for poor voters.

courts. District court judge Lynn Adelman invalidated the law in May 2014, saying it disproportionately affected black and Hispanic voters who were less likely to possess driver's licenses. Adelman also noted that the law was unnecessary:

> No evidence suggests that voter-impersonation fraud will become a problem at any time in the foreseeable future. . . . A person would have to be insane to commit voter-impersonation fraud. The potential costs of perpetrating the fraud, which include a $10,000 fine and three years of imprisonment, are extremely high in comparison to the potential benefits, which would be nothing more than one additional vote for a preferred candidate . . . a vote which is unlikely to change the election's outcome.[22]

Robin Vos, the Republican speaker of the Wisconsin State Assembly, opposed Adelman's ruling because the judge had

Voter ID Laws Ensure the Integrity of the Voting Process

Jonathan S. Tobin, the chief political blogger for the conservative publication *Commentary*, defends voter ID laws as commonsense protection to ensure the integrity of elections:

> Assuring the integrity of the voting process is something that most citizens instinctively understand is the right thing to do. In the America of 2012, you need a picture ID to get on a plane, ride Amtrak [trains], open a bank account, perform any transaction with most businesses and government, as well as buy alcohol or tobacco.
>
> Why is voting less important? States must preserve the integrity of the ballot process, especially in an era of close elections. . . . Yet opponents of voter ID laws paint them as racist, meant to suppress the minorities. . . . That's a canard [myth]. There's nothing racist about a procedure that can help prevent people who aren't citizens or who aren't legally registered from committing fraud. . . .
>
> As for liberal assertions that there is no voter fraud in the United States, most Americans respond with a snicker. To believe that the parties and their supporters don't try to cheat requires us to ignore American political history—as well as just about everything we know about human nature.

Jonathan S. Tobin, "3 Views on Whether US States Should Require Voter ID," *Christian Science Monitor*, October 2, 2012. www.csmonitor.com.

been appointed to his position in 1997 by Democratic president Bill Clinton. Vos believed Adelman's ruling was politically motivated: "He used his personal bias to say that voter ID is just wrong. . . . Our intention was never to make it hard to vote. All we want to do is make sure we have some reasonable proof that people are who they say they are."[23]

Wisconsin appealed the decision to the Seventh Circuit Court, which reversed Adelman's ruling. This allowed Act 23 to go back into effect less than two months before the November 2014 midterm elections. The law faced other court challenges but remained in place during the 2016 presidential election when Donald Trump beat Hillary Clinton in Wisconsin by a margin of 22,748 votes. A 2017 study by the voter advocacy group Priorities USA found that

Voter ID Laws Suppress Nonwhite Voting

Peter Lindsay is a professor of political science at Georgia State University. In the following commentary, Lindsay questions the motives of those who support voter ID laws:

Are you racist? One way to find out is to ask yourself what you think about the various voter identification laws that are now in effect in 33 states. . . . Voter ID laws do not make voting less fraudulent (because there is no fraud to prevent). . . . Why, then, do people support them? There are two possibilities. First, people could actually wish to suppress non-white voting. . . . Of course, some Republican partisans might wish to suppress non-white voting because it leans Democratic. Their anti-democratic motivation may not technically be racist, but as the effect of their efforts clearly is.

This brings us to the second possible explanation for why people support voter ID laws: They are mistaken about the facts. Either they think voter fraud is a problem, or they don't see the ways strict voter ID laws prevent blacks, Hispanics and Asian-Americans from voting—or both. And so we return to my opening question, with a new twist: If you support voter ID laws, are you a racist or just misinformed?

Peter Lindsay, "Are You Racist? Let's Look at Your Position on Voter ID," *Hill*, October 10, 2016. http://thehill.com.

Donald Trump and Hillary Clinton debate during the 2016 presidential campaign. Voting rights advocates felt that Wisconsin's strict ID law helped Trump win the state by a slim margin.

Act 23 suppressed voter turnout by 200,000 votes during that election. Many voting rights advocates felt that Wisconsin's strict ID law helped swing the election in Trump's favor. Investigative reporter Ari Berman wrote that this would be impossible to prove. But Berman faulted the media for ignoring the issue: "We'll likely never know how many people were kept from the polls by restrictions like voter-ID laws . . . and barriers to voter registration. But at the very least this should have been a question that many more people were looking into [before the election]."[24]

North Carolina's HB 589

North Carolina is another state where Republican legislators changed long-standing laws that governed voting rights. In 2013 North Carolina's legislature passed House Bill (HB) 589, which enacted many new election rules one month after the Supreme Court struck down Section 4 of the Voting Rights Act. This provision previously required forty North Carolina counties to seek federal approval before changing their voting laws. After Republican governor Pat McCrory signed HB 589, he stated, "While some will try to make this seem to be controversial, the simple reality is that requiring voters to provide a photo ID when they vote is a common-sense idea. This new law brings our state in line with a healthy majority of other states throughout the country. This common-sense safeguard is commonplace."[25]

McCrory and other supporters of the photo ID bill pointed out that a large majority of the public supports such laws. According to a 2012 poll by the *Washington Post*, nearly three-quarters of Americans believe that people should have to show photo identification to vote. Additionally, about half of all Americans believe that voter fraud is a major problem. Among Republicans, two-thirds believe that voter fraud is a problem.

Although North Carolina lawmakers cited voter fraud as justification for HB 589, a lawsuit filed by a voter rights organization later revealed the origin of the bill. North Carolina legislators crafted the measure on the basis of state voter data they had obtained in 2012. Lawmakers broke down voter turnout by race. The Republican Speaker of the House specifically asked for statistics about registered voters who did not possess a license to drive, which primarily singled out poor black citizens. Based on this data about voter behavior, legislators crafted HB 589 to require specific forms of ID that minorities were less likely to possess.

Cutting Early Voting Hours

Another section of North Carolina's voter bill cut down the period of early voting from seventeen to ten days. During early voting periods, voters can cast their ballots before election day, either by mail or at selected polling places. The process is meant to encourage voting and ease crowding at polling places on election day. When there are fewer early voting days available, polls are more crowded, and people with busy schedules find it more difficult to cast their ballots. North Carolina lawmakers also eliminated same-day voter registration, a practice that allows citizens to register and vote at the same time on early voting days. As with their support for voter IDs, lawmakers argued that same-day registration and early voting encourage fraud. As Dallas Woodhouse, the leader of North Carolina's Republican Party, stated in 2016, "We believe same-day registration is ripe with voter fraud, or the opportunity to commit it. Same-day registration is only available during early voting. We are under no obligation to offer more opportunities for voter fraud."[26]

> "We believe same-day registration is ripe with voter fraud, or the opportunity to commit it. . . . We are under no obligation to offer more opportunities for voter fraud."[26]
>
> —Dallas Woodhouse, the leader of North Carolina's Republican Party

Critics and independent analysts could find no proof to back up Woodhouse's statement. However, data does show that cutting early voting hours deters people from voting. In 2012 Florida cut early voting from fourteen days to eight days. Fewer available days for voting led to long lines at the polls, with up to seven-hour lines at polling places in big cities like Miami, where Democrats are a majority. A 2013 study by the *Orlando Sentinel* newspaper showed that at least 210,000 voters gave up in frustration due to the long lines.

North Carolina Republicans were aware of Florida's situation when they cut early voting days in 2013. Politicians also made it harder for young voters to cast a ballot by eliminating polling places on college campuses. Some observers maintain that African Americans were targeted by the law that eliminated Sunday voting. Traditionally, African American churches organize events called Souls to the Polls on Sundays before an election. After services, church members are bused to their local polling place to cast a ballot. Journalist William Wan offered his opinion of the law: "North Carolina [Republican] leaders launched a meticulous and coordinated effort to deter black voters, who overwhelmingly vote for Democrats. The law, created and passed entirely by white legislators, evoked the state's ugly history of blocking

African Americans from voting—practices that had taken a civil rights movement and extensive federal intervention to stop."[27]

North Carolina's new voting laws were challenged in court. In 2016 the US Court of Appeals for the Fourth Circuit invalidated the restrictions in HB 589. The court decision explained that the Republicans wrote the bill to "target African-Americans with almost surgical precision."[28] According to the appeals court, the law violated the Voting Rights Act and the Fourteenth Amendment. The ruling also pointed out that the Republicans had "failed to identify even a single individual who has ever been charged with committing in-person voter fraud in North Carolina."[29] North Carolina Republicans appealed the ruling to the Supreme Court, but the court refused to hear the case. The state's Republicans then vowed they would enact new voting restrictions.

An Inalienable Right

Critics often hold up North Carolina and Wisconsin as the most extreme examples of voter suppression. Yet by 2016 strict voter ID laws were in effect in thirty-three states. The US Congress could fix some of these problems by setting minimum standards for state elections. For example, Congress could pass a law allowing automatic voter registration when voters turn eighteen. However, Congress has shown little interest in meddling with state election laws.

While the debate continues, voting rights advocates can point to the Declaration of Independence to bolster their cause. It says governments derive "their power from the consent of the governed" and all Americans have "certain unalienable rights." Nowhere does the Declaration of Independence or the US Constitution say that politicians have the right to choose who gets to vote and on what days and hours they are allowed to exercise that right. Voting is considered an inalienable right for all American citizens. As Roy Cooper said after being elected North Carolina's governor in 2016, "We need to be making it easier to vote, not harder."[30]

CHAPTER 3

Polling Place Problems

During the 2016 presidential election, over 126 million Americans cast a ballot, many at their local polling place. This required a massive, coordinated effort by thousands of election officials who set up voting machines and supervised the election in more than 113,000 polling stations. Americans voted in schools, libraries, fire stations, churches, town halls, and even in surf shops, laundromats, and restaurants. These polling places are located in more than 174,000 precincts, also called "voting districts." (Sometimes a precinct has more than one polling place, and sometimes voters from several precincts will visit a single polling place.)

Although presidential elections receive the most public attention, election officials work year-round. National elections are held every two years. Primary elections are held in the spring or summer, depending on the state. Candidates selected in the primary face off in a general election held in November. In many places, local and state elections are held during odd-numbered years.

Like many other aspects of government, elections have become highly politicized. Elections in the United States are generally overseen by local officials who follow varying rules and procedures depending on the state and county where they are located. Even though there is a great deal of variation in the way elections are conducted from place to place, election officials have one overriding task: to ensure that citizens can vote as quickly and efficiently as possible. However, some have been accused of using tactics to make voting as difficult as possible for some groups, including minorities, the disabled, the young, the elderly, and non-English-speakers.

Arizona's Voting Fiasco

During Arizona's primary election in March 2016, election officials made national headlines when they limited the number of polling places in some precincts during the election. Although Arizona is a Republican-dominated state, Phoenix, located in Maricopa County, has a Democratic majority. In 2016 a Republican election official, Helen Purcell, reduced the number of polling places in Maricopa County by 70 percent. In 2012 the county ran two hundred polling places; however, in 2016 officials provided only sixty, or one polling place per 21,000 registered voters. But even within Maricopa County, election officials appeared to favor some areas over others. In Cave Creek, which is primarily white, there was one polling place per 8,500 residents. In Phoenix, which is 41 percent Hispanic, there was only one polling place per 108,000 residents. The problems at the polls were predictable. Long lines formed and voters were discouraged.

At one polling place near downtown Phoenix, up to seven hundred voters waited in the 80°F heat in a line that spooled along four city blocks. Throughout the city, voters were forced to wait up to seven hours to enter their polling places. Countless voters left in frustration without casting ballots. Finding parking near the polling places also was difficult; some voters reported searching for parking places for more than thirty minutes before giving up. Leslie Feldman was one voter who was impacted by the polling place problems at the Church of the Beatitudes in Phoenix. Feldman, who waited in line for more than four hours with her three-year-old daughter and twelve-week-old baby, described the experience:

> The church was clearly not equipped to handle the thousands of people who were required to vote there. So many

people needed use the bathroom that it got backed up and there was sewage leaking onto the grass where we were all waiting. We were snaking around the sewage. It was absolutely ridiculous. . . . When I got [to the front of the line], I was told there were no ballots left for Democrats. . . . The stack of ballots for Republicans was over a foot high. For the very first time in my life, I was starting to feel disenfranchised.[31]

Feldman was directed to another polling place, where Democratic ballots were available. She was able to cast her ballot at 8:05 pm after first arriving at a polling place at 3:20. Such problems were not limited to Maricopa County. Pima County, which is 35 percent Latino, lost sixty-two polling places in 2016, more than any other county in the nation. Cochise County, located along the Mexican border, closed thirty-one polling places, leaving only eighteen for its 130,000 residents.

Democratic state senator Martin Quezada of Arizona says long lines create a sense of distrust in the system among people of color and can keep people away from the polls: "If [Hispanic voters] don't have a good experience on Election Day when they are casting their ballot, their likelihood of participating in a system they don't trust again in the future becomes that much harder."[32]

The voting situation in Arizona can be compared to that of neighboring California, a majority Democratic state. Election officials in California have worked to reduce the wait time at the polls. Before the 2016 elections, they analyzed election-related data, including the number of registered voters in each county, historic voter turnout, the capacity of each polling place, and even the

> "The [polling place] was clearly not equipped to handle the thousands of people who were required to vote there. . . . For the very first time in my life, I was starting to feel disenfranchised."[31]
>
> —Arizona voter Leslie Feldman

In the 2016 presidential election, over 126 million Americans cast a ballot. This required a massive effort by election officials and volunteers to manage more than 113,000 polling stations throughout the country.

number of available parking spots. Guided by this information, officials assigned poll workers, distributed ballots, and directed voters to specific polling locations. This sophisticated technique drastically lowered wait times at California polls. According to Michael Scarpello, the registrar of voters in San Bernardino County, "If there are lines, they are short. At most, voters wait five minutes. . . . Our job is to make voting as convenient as possible for voters. If voters are motivated, we don't want to put any barriers in their way."[33]

> "Our job is to make voting as convenient as possible for voters. If voters are motivated, we don't want to put any barriers in their way."[33]
>
> —Michael Scarpello, the registrar of voters for San Bernardino County, California

Shutting Polling Places Across the South

Arizona has a long history of voter discrimination. It was one of the states required by Section 5 of the Voting Rights Act to seek federal approval for changes in its voting practices. After the Supreme Court struck down key sections of the act in 2013,

37

Fewer Polling Places Disenfranchise Voters

In 2013 the Supreme Court struck down key provisions of the Voting Rights Act in the court case *Shelby County v. Holder*. As a result, 868 polling places were closed, many in minority neighborhoods. The Leadership Conference Education Fund studied the damaging effects of the *Shelby* decision in a report excerpted below.

> Polling place closures are a particularly common and pernicious tactic for disenfranchising voters of color. Decisions to shutter or reduce voting locations are often made quietly and at the last minute. . . . These changes can place an undue burden on minority voters, who may be less likely to have access to public transportation or vehicles. . . .
>
> Once an election is conducted, there is no judicial remedy for the loss of votes that were never cast because a voter's usual polling place has disappeared. Pre-Shelby, jurisdictions were required to give substantial notice to voters about any planned polling place closures. . . . Post-Shelby, voters have to rely on news reports and anecdotes from local advocates who attend city and county commission meetings or legislative sessions where these changes are contemplated to identify potentially discriminatory polling place location and precinct changes. In the vast majority of instances, closures have gone unnoticed, unreported, and unchallenged.

Scott Simpson, "The Great Poll Closure," Leadership Conference Education Fund, 2016. http://civilrights docs.info.

Arizona was free to reduce the number of polling places without prior approval. Critics say this was part of a growing trend to restrict voter access. In 2016 the Leadership Conference Education Fund, a civil rights group, studied 381 counties previously covered by Section 5. Forty-three percent of those counties—165 in all—reduced voting locations. As a result, 868 polling places that had been open to voters in 2014 disappeared in 2016. Louisi-

Fewer Polling Places Save Taxpayers Money

Former election official Phil Keisling explains that the March 2016 polling place closures in Arizona were not a shadowy conspiracy to disenfranchise voters. Polls were closed simply to save money.

> When Arizona legislators decided to create a separate, stand-alone presidential primary election, they promised counties full reimbursement. But costs soon outstripped legislative appetites. This year, Maricopa County estimated it would cost about $3.5 million to hold another 200-polling-place election. This was about $1 million more than the state's reimbursement formula allowed. . . . Meanwhile, more and more voters were avoiding polling places altogether, preferring the convenience of mailed-out absentee ballots. . . . March's long lines obscured [the] fact that . . . 535,000 voters (85 percent of the total) used [mail-in] ballots.
>
> Maricopa officials obviously failed to strike that optimal balance. A relative handful—maybe a dozen—of the sites were unexpectedly overloaded with far more voters than projected. Hence some intolerably long lines, and a spate of bad publicity that Arizona's other counties largely avoided. [But] Maricopa's election officials deserve at least two cheers of praise for getting it *almost* right this time—and some encouragement to continue to try to make voting more accessible as well as more cost-effective for as many voters as possible.

Phil Keisling, "The Wrong Lesson from the Voting Fiasco," *Governing*, July 12, 2016. www.governing.com.

ana closed 103 polling places; Mississippi, 44; Alabama, 66; and North Carolina, 27.

Only in one southern state are voters protected from the negative effects of poll closures. South Carolina has legal requirements for changes to election laws that guarantee transparency. Although the state eliminated 12 polling places in 2016, this was only 1 percent of the total. Additionally, South Carolina's election

In Tempe, Arizona, voters enter and exit their polling station to vote in the 2016 presidential election. Arizona has a long history of voter discrimination.

law says that any polling place changes must be approved by the state legislator who represents the precinct. The law also requires that voters in the altered precinct be notified of the change in writing, typically in the form of a letter mailed to every registered voter. Additionally, any proposed changes must be posted on the state's election commission website. According to South Carolina voting activist Brett Bursey, "This won't keep bad things from happening. But at least voters and advocacy groups will be given notice before [polling place closures] take effect."[34] Bursey believes that this combination of transparency and providing notice has prevented officials from following the trend of widespread polling place closures seen in other states.

A Shift to Vote Centers

Texas leads the nation in the number of polling place closures. In 2016 state officials shut down at least 403 polling places, many in counties with black and Hispanic majorities. In some counties, voter websites provided polling place information before the 2016 election. But dozens of Texas counties failed to provide information about voting changes in Spanish as well as English. Scott Simpson, the author of the Leadership Conference Education Fund study, explained the problem: "These precincts didn't even have Spanish-language material in their websites. . . . How are you going to inform [Spanish-speaking voters] about significant changes in voting practices?"[35]

Texas officials claim that the polling place closures were part of a plan to institute a new type of streamlined voting at places called vote centers or superprecincts. Rather than have citizens vote at their local neighborhood polls, Texas voters could cast their ballots in any vote center in their county of residence. Michelle Bennett, the elections administrator of Aransas County, explains why this is a positive development: "It actually makes it easier for voters to vote because they can vote anywhere on Election Day without having to go to a specific poll site. Previously, if they went to the wrong poll site and they weren't in that precinct, they'd be directed to the precinct they were registered in. Now we don't turn anybody away."[36]

Those who promote vote centers point out that this new system can save millions of dollars. Only two states, Alaska and Delaware, pay the election costs incurred by local governments. In most states, including Texas and Arizona, expenses such as paying poll workers are picked up by the county. Additionally, there has been a dramatic increase in the number of residents voting early or voting by mail. As a result, fewer polling places are needed. However, the Leadership Conference Education Fund issues the following warning regarding this shift away from neighborhood voting: "In some instances, reducing polling places and converting to vote centers is justified as a possible means to increase voter turnout. Without Section 5, there are no protections for voters of color to ensure that when reductions are made for seemingly reasonable purposes, they do not disadvantage voters of color."[37]

Hacking the Vote

Although citizens and activists can fight poll closures, another threat to voting rights is more insidious and harder to prevent. Millions of Americans cast their ballots on voting machines that were manufactured during the early twenty-first century. The voting machines use technology considered ancient by modern standards, and they are shockingly easy to hack. The issue made headlines in 2017 when hackers at the DEFCON cybersecurity conference in Las Vegas entered a competition to break into voting machines.

DEFCON sponsors set up what they called the Voting Machine Hacking Village. The site contained thirty different voting machines like those used in recent elections. As tech writer Kevin Roose states, the machines "ran on comically outdated software."[38] Within minutes hackers were able to break into the machines and manipulate the software to register fake voters and change vote totals. Hackers found one machine, the AVS WinVote model, with a security flaw from 2003. This means that the entire time the machine was in use—since 2003—it could be controlled remotely by a person not on the premises. That person could observe which candidate a voter was selecting and change the vote or shut down the system entirely. The same machine had an unchangeable default user name—admin—and password—abcde. Hackers discovered this using a simple Google search.

DEFCON hackers found obvious problems in other voting machines. Many were manufactured with parts made in China. This means there is no security in the supply chain; the machines could possibly be hacked before they even roll off the assembly line. Computer security expert Matt Blaze, who organized the Voting Machine Hacking Village, explains how foreign agents could tamper with machines made in other nations: "A nation-state actor with resources, expertise and motive—like Russia—could exploit these supply chain security flaws to plant malware into the parts of every machine, and indeed could breach vast segments of U.S. election infrastructure remotely, all at once."[39]

At the DEFCON cybersecurity conference in 2017, sponsors set up a competition called the Voting Machine Hacking Village to demonstrate how easily currently used voting machines can be hacked.

Blaze's concern was heightened by a report by the Department of Homeland Security (DHS). In 2017 the DHS revealed that Russian hackers had attempted to infiltrate election networks in twenty-one states during the 2016 presidential election. Shadowy foreign agents are not the only ones who can take advantage of security holes in voting machines, however. The task would be even simpler for political insiders who could ostensibly work undercover at American companies that program the machines. Voting machines could also be hacked by political operatives who visit polling places on election day. One common voting machine, the Sequoia AVC Advantage, is widely used in Pennsylvania, New Jersey, and Virginia. The Sequoia can be altered in minutes by a hacker using only a screwdriver. A voter using the altered machine could cast a ballot for one candidate but the software would register a vote for a different candidate.

Although the flaws found in voting machines are real, there is no evidence that anyone has ever executed a successful election hack. And officials are increasingly imposing tight security measures that restrict who has access to voting equipment. However, old voting machines will remain a target to those who might wish to challenge the integrity of American elections. As J. Alex Halderman, a professor of computer science, says, "Even if the 2016 election wasn't hacked, the 2020 election might well be."[40]

Old Machines Open to Manipulation

The problem with voting machines goes back to the presidential election held in 2000 between Al Gore and George W. Bush. The election was so close that the decision of who would become president of the United States came down to a few hundred votes cast in Florida. One of the most enduring images from that election is that of a Florida election official peering at a damaged paper ballot trying to determine the voter's intention. Almost five weeks after the election, Bush was pronounced the winner by a margin of 537 votes.

After the election fiasco, a joint study by the Massachusetts Institute of Technology and the California Institute of Technology revealed a wide range of polling place problems. On election day in 2000, faulty voting machines, damaged paper ballots, and other polling place issues resulted in 1.5 to 2 million lost votes. The study spurred political action. In October 2002 Congress passed the Help America Vote Act, which provided states with more than $2 billion to replace obsolete voting machines and paper ballots. The vast majority of voting machines throughout the United States were replaced by the time of the November 2004 presidential election. In many cases, old systems were replaced by electronic devices known as Direct Recording Election (DRE) voting machines. Although this was good news at the time, it is bad news today; thousands of DRE voting machines are still in use.

DRE voting machines are computers that run on laptop technology developed during the 1990s. They use touch screens to record votes; users view ballots on a screen and make their selections by touching a box next to a candidate's name. Votes are stored on a memory card or compact disc. Some can broadcast votes using a modem or Wi-Fi connection that sends vote totals to a central database, where they are compiled and counted.

DRE and other aged digital voting machines were used in forty-three states during the 2016 presidential election. These machines are a security risk. They run on outdated software like Windows XP and Windows 2000. These operating systems are no longer supported by Microsoft, which means they do not receive security updates. As election fraud expert Jonathan Simon explains,

> "Computerized vote counting, taking place in the pitch-dark of cyberspace, is an open invitation to manipulation and election theft, by outsiders and even more likely by insiders."[41]
>
> —Jonathan Simon, an election fraud expert

Computerized vote counting, taking place in the pitch-dark of cyberspace, is an open invitation to manipulation and election theft, by outsiders and even more likely by insiders with easy access. . . . If the touchscreen or scanner or central tabulator "made a mistake" or was programmed to delete your vote or flip it to a different candidate invisibly, you would have no idea that this had happened. Thousands, ultimately millions, of votes could be affected without knowledge of voters or election officials.[41]

When voting machines are vulnerable to tampering, the voting rights of all citizens are threatened. Hacked machines can cause people to lose confidence in the security of the voting process. By sowing distrust, enemies of the United States can suppress voter turnout and cause voters to question the legitimacy of the winning candidate. With foreign interests and other malicious actors attempting to hack America's voting infrastructure, upgrading these outdated systems is critical for protecting voters' rights.

Purging Voter Rolls

In 2011 army veteran Joe Helle returned to his hometown of Oak Harbor, Ohio, after serving tours in Iraq and Afghanistan. When Helle tried to vote in a local election, he was turned away. A poll worker told Helle that his name could not be found on the voter roll, also known as the voter registration list. Like every other state, Ohio maintains voter rolls that contain the names of every registered voter. On election day, poll workers use voter rolls to verify the identity of individual voters and ensure they are eligible to vote in their state.

Ohio has very strict voter rules concerning what is called inactivity. Voters who do not cast ballots every two years receive a notice in the mail. If they do not respond to the notice or fail to vote in the following four years, their names are purged (eliminated) from the state voter rolls. Helle's name was removed from the voter rolls for inactivity; he had not responded to the letter or voted within the designated period. The law made no exception for active duty military personnel—Helle was deployed overseas during the period in question and says he never received any notification. In 2018 Helle described how he felt after learning his name had been removed from the voter rolls: "I started crying. To come home after defending that fundamental right [to vote] and to be told that I couldn't exercise it, that was heartbreaking. . . . [I] could not exercise it because of this archaic, terrible policy."[42]

Use It or Lose It

Ohio's system of purging names from voter rolls is referred to as the use-it-or-lose-it policy. Supporters of the policy say it prevents voter fraud and ensures the integrity of the electoral process. By purging names, the state helps reduce the risk of fraud by eliminating potentially deceased individuals. This prevents cheaters from using the names of the dead to cast fraudulent votes. The process also removes the names of voters who have moved and registered elsewhere. Purging their names would prevent them from possibly casting ballots in two separate locations.

Every state regularly cleans its voter rolls, but only a few follow Ohio's strict policy, which effectively purges any voter

"To come home after defending that fundamental right [to vote] and to be told that I couldn't exercise it, that was heartbreaking."[42]

—Ohio voter and veteran Joe Helle

who failed to vote in a single presidential election. Between 2011 and 2016, Ohio purged 1.2 million names for inactivity. Purges include members of all political parties. However, according to a 2016 analysis by Reuters, voters from Democrat-leaning neighborhoods are twice as likely to be struck from voter rolls as those in Republican areas. In Cuyahoga County, for example, neighborhoods that backed Barack Obama in 2012 saw 5 percent of their voters purged. In neighborhoods that backed Obama's Republican opponent, John McCain, only 2.5 percent of registered voters were removed for inactivity. Similar numbers were seen in Franklin County and Hamilton County. Part of the discrepancy is due to the way local election officials chose to implement the law. In rural counties with fewer voters, election officials spend more time checking into the status of voters before removing them from the rolls. In populous Cuyahoga County, computers flag thousands of names every year, leaving busy officials to automatically purge names of those who do not regularly vote.

The purges are also affected by trends in voter behavior. According to the Reuters study, which was based on historical election turnouts, Republicans are more likely to vote in midterm elections held every two years and presidential elections held every four years. Democrats are more likely to vote only in presidential contests. According to Republican John Husted, Ohio's secretary of state, people who do not regularly vote should not complain: "If this is really [an] important thing to you in your life, voting, you probably would have done so within a six-year period."[43] Democratic state representative Kathleen Clyde does not agree: "You shouldn't be struck of your right to vote because you skipped an election."[44]

Surging Numbers

Although Ohio's policy of removing the names of infrequent voters is unique, secretaries of state across the nation are legally required to purge names from voter lists on a regular basis. Recently, though, the task has become more difficult as the number of registered voters has surged. When Obama first ran for president in 2008 there were around 146 million registered voters in the nation; by 2016 there were over 200 million voters. The population of the United States increased by around 6 percent during Obama's eight years in office, but the number of people registered to vote surged 33 percent.

"You shouldn't be struck of your right to vote because you skipped an election."[44]

—Democratic state representative Kathleen Clyde

Any list containing millions of names is bound to contain errors and duplications, and voter rolls are no exception. About 40 million Americans move each year, and many reregister to vote in their new locations without canceling their old voter registrations. As a result, around 2.75 million Americans are registered in more than one state, according to a 2012 study by the Pew Research Center. Additionally, the names of nearly 2 million dead people remain on voter rolls.

Congress addressed the voter roll issues in 2002 when the Help America Vote Act (HAVA) was passed. The law established new administration standards for federal elections. HAVA requires states to maintain computerized voter registration databases that are accurate and updated regularly. (The federal government does not maintain a national voter registration database.) HAVA guidelines require states to check voter rolls against postal service

The population of the United States increased around 6 percent during President Obama's eight years in office. However, during the same period, the number of registered voters surged 33 percent.

change-of-address information to find voters who have moved. States also consult the Social Security Death Index database, which lists the names of people who die every year.

State and county officials use HAVA guidelines to periodically purge names from voter rolls. When done properly, these purges help make the voting system more efficient while instilling a sense of integrity in the system; no one wants the names of dead or ineligible voters to clutter up registration rolls. But eligible voters are inevitably kicked off the rolls because the process is not perfect. And most of these voters do not know their names have been purged until they attempt to cast ballots on election day.

Cross-Checking Names

One method commonly used to purge voter rolls is also a source of widespread controversy. A computer program called the Interstate

Crosscheck Targets Voter Fraud

Hans A. von Spakovsky is an elections expert who alleges that thousands of people voted more than once in the 2016 presidential election. Spakovsky based his conclusion on a study by the conservative Government Accountability Institute.

> Over the last few months, the [Government Accountability] Institute sought to obtain "public voter information" from [seventeen states] in order to search for duplicate votes. . . . [The institute] found that 8,471 votes in 2016 were "highly likely" duplicates. Extrapolating this to all 50 states would likely produce, with "high-confidence," around 45,000 duplicate votes. . . . The probability of 45,000 illegal duplicate votes is the low end of the spectrum, and it does not even account for other types of fraud such as ineligible voting by noncitizens and felons and absentee ballot fraud.
>
> To put this number of fraudulent votes in perspective, Hillary Clinton won New Hampshire [in 2016] by fewer than 3,000 votes out of over 700,000 cast. Just this number of duplicate votes alone has the power to swing state results and, in turn, elections. . . . All of this is just the latest evidence that we have serious, substantive problems in our voter registration system across the country and that voter fraud is, without a doubt, real.

Hans A. von Spakovsky, "New Report Exposes Thousands of Illegal Votes in 2016 Election," Heritage Foundation, July 28, 2017. www.heritage.org.

Voter Registration Crosscheck Program, or simply Crosscheck, compiles names of voters who are allegedly registered in more than one state, typically because people move periodically. The free service combines the voter rolls of each participating state into a huge database. A computer program searches for duplicate registrations based on first name, last name, and date of birth. Crosscheck was first used in three midwestern states in 2006, and the program expanded rapidly in the years that followed. In

Crosscheck Targets Democratic Voters

Greg Palast is an investigative journalist who specializes in voting rights. In 2016 Palast wrote the following analysis of the Interstate Voter Registration Crosscheck Program used in twenty-eight states to purge names from voter rolls:

> When Donald Trump claimed [in 2016], "the election's going to be rigged," he wasn't entirely wrong. But the threat was not, as Trump warned, from Americans committing the crime of "voting many, many times." What's far more likely to undermine democracy . . . is the culmination of a decade-long Republican effort to disenfranchise voters under the guise of battling voter fraud. The latest tool [is] . . . the Interstate Voter Registration Crosscheck Program, which is being promoted by a powerful Republican operative [Kris Kobach], and its lists of potential duplicate voters are kept confidential. But [my team] obtained a portion of the list and the names of 1 million targeted voters. According to our analysis, the Crosscheck list disproportionately threatens solid Democratic constituencies: young, black, Hispanic and Asian-American voters. . . . Low voter turnout of any kind traditionally favors the [Republicans], and this is the party's long game to keep the rolls free of young people, minorities and the poor.

Greg Palast, "The GOP's Stealth War Against Voters," *Rolling Stone*, August 24, 2016. www.rollingstone .com.

2017 election officials in twenty-eight states used Crosscheck to analyze 98 million voter registrations. The program found 7.2 million names it classified as potential duplicate registrants. Nearly all of these double registrations were unintentional, a result of people who moved and reregistered to vote.

Crosscheck has two purposes. The first is to identify people registered in more than one state. The second purpose is to identify possible duplicate voters, or people who have voted two times in different places. These duplicate voters could theoretically cast a ballot in one state and travel to a second state and vote again. Supporters of Crosscheck say it prevents this potential crime.

Crosscheck has been the subject of heated political debate because Kris Kobach, a lawyer and powerful Republican politician, directed its creation and oversees its operation. Kobach, who served as Kansas's secretary of state from 2010 to 2018, has made numerous controversial statements about the rare crime of voter fraud in the United States. In 2010 Kobach stated that two thousand voters used the identities of dead people to illegally vote in Kansas elections. Journalists who investigated the claim found it to be completely false. Kobach also supported President Trump's claim that millions of noncitizens had voted in the 2016 election. This claim has also been repeatedly debunked by numerous scholars and reporters who investigated the charge. Kobach's statements and political positions have left many Democrats to question the justification for using Crosscheck.

> "[Crosscheck] illustrates how a successful multistate effort can be in enhancing the integrity of our elections and in keeping our voter rolls accurate."[45]
>
> —Kris Kobach, Kansas's secretary of state

In 2017 Kobach said Crosscheck "illustrates how successful a multistate effort can be in enhancing the integrity of our elections and in keeping our voter rolls accurate."[45] Kobach also has used the program to convict nine Kansas residents for voting twice between 2010 and 2017. Critics point out that around 7 million ballots were cast in Kansas elections held during this period, which means only 0.00012 percent were double voters, an insignificant number to affect an election.

Kobach has a team of eight administrators working on double-voter prosecutions. One of the targets was a sixty-seven-year-old rancher named Que J. Fullmer, who owns ranches in Kansas and Colorado. In November 2016 Fullmer cast votes for state and local representatives in both states. Fullmer justified his double voting by saying he pays taxes in both states and feels he should be

Kris Kobach (on right), seen here with President Trump in 2017, directed the creation and implementation of Crosscheck, a system designed to eliminate duplicate voting. Kobach also supported Trump's false claim that millions of noncitizens voted in the 2016 election.

represented in local and state races in both places. Fullmer, a Republican, only voted for his preferred presidential candidate in Kansas. When Crosscheck flagged Fullmer's name, Kobach charged him with four felonies that included voting without being qualified, voting more than once, and advancing unlawful acts while voting. Fullmer paid a stiff fine and was placed on probation for two years.

Almost every other person Kobach prosecuted was a white Republican over the age of sixty who owned land in two states. Several of the senior citizens he prosecuted said they did not understand that it was illegal to vote in two states. Kobach secured $30,000 total in fines from all the double voters. In an official press release from 2017, Kobach announced that these convictions demonstrate "how prevalent the crime of double voting is. In Kansas, we are making it clear that people who willfully vote twice will be prosecuted. This is an important part of our effort to make Kansas elections the most secure in the nation."[46]

Faulty Methods

Kobach's critics say his focus on double voting is a waste of money and state resources. Researchers argue that the method Crosscheck uses to detect potential duplicate registrants is highly inaccurate. The program uses only two data points—name and date of birth—to identify a voter. In 2017 researchers at Stanford, Harvard, the University of Pennsylvania, and Microsoft examined national voter files. They found there is a fifty-fifty chance that in any group of 180 people, two of those people will share the exact same birthdate—day, month, and year. And in any election, names like William Smith and Maria Rodriguez show up hundreds of times. In New Jersey, for example, 282 people named William Smith cast a ballot in 2004. Odds are that two might share the exact same birthday and both would be flagged as double voters by Crosscheck. The study concluded that the purging strategies used by Crosscheck would eliminate three hundred valid registered voters for every purported double vote it prevented. Put another way, over 99 percent of the purged names were unlikely to be associated with voter fraud.

Journalist Greg Palast, who specializes in voting rights issues, examined Crosscheck results from another perspective. In 2016 Palast analyzed a list of 1 million names targeted by Crosscheck. He found that around one-fourth of the people on the list had similar first and last names but different middle names. According to a Georgia list from Crosscheck, James Brown was suspected of double voting 357 times. And the system listed James Arthur Brown, James Clifford Brown, and James Lynn Brown as the same person. Additionally, the system ignored fathers and sons with the same name who use the designation *senior* and *junior*.

Palast worked with database expert Mark Swedlund, whose clients include eBay and American Express. Swedlund conducted a statistical analysis that showed that African American, Hispanic, and Asian American names were overrepresented on Crosscheck rolls. This is not surprising. According to the US Census Bureau, minorities have eighty-five of the one hundred most common last names. If a person is named Washington, there is an 89 percent chance that he or she is African American. If someone is named Hernandez, there is a 94 percent chance that he or she is Hispanic. Ninety-five percent of the people with the last name Kim are Asian. Swedlund said he was shocked by the system's "childish methodology," adding, "God forbid your name is Garcia, of which there are 858,000 in the U.S., and your first name is Joseph or Jose. You're probably suspected of voting in 27 states."[47]

> "I can't tell you what the intent was. I can only tell you what the outcome is. And the outcome is discriminatory against minorities."[48]
>
> —Database expert Mark Swedlund

The Crosscheck methodology marks one in six Hispanics as potential duplicate voters. One in nine African Americans would land on the list, as would one in seven Asian Americans. When asked if Crosscheck deliberately targeted minorities, Swedlund replied, "I'm a data guy. I can't tell you what the intent was. I can only tell you what the outcome is. And the outcome is discriminatory against minorities."[48]

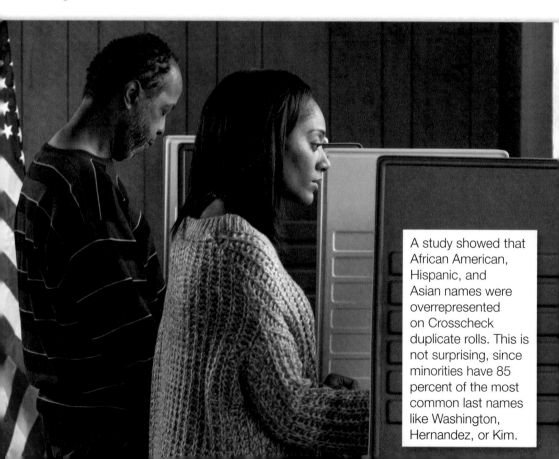

A study showed that African American, Hispanic, and Asian names were overrepresented on Crosscheck duplicate rolls. This is not surprising, since minorities have 85 percent of the most common last names like Washington, Hernandez, or Kim.

Doing What the Law Requires

With critics and government officials clashing over Crosscheck, the battle over voter rolls is sure to continue. In November 2017 a conservative advocacy group called the Public Interest Legal Foundation (PILF) sent a notice to 248 county election boards stating that federal law required the officials to purge their voter rolls. If any officials failed to do so, they could become the target of a federal lawsuit filed by PILF. When asked about the lawsuit threat, PILF's president, J. Christian Adams, responded, "It seems like we've arrived to the point where asking election officials to do what the law requires makes PILF subversive."[49]

PILF is among several conservative groups, including Judicial Watch, the American Civil Rights Union, and True the Vote, that are working to purge voter rolls. Voting rights advocates and most Democratic election officials say that the purges are a threat to voting rights. They are intended to reduce the number of minority, poor, and young voters who are disproportionately Democrats. Elections supervisor Brenda Snipes, who oversees elections in Florida's Democratic stronghold, Broward County, received a threatening PILF letter. According to Snipes, groups like PILF "target minority areas and heavily Democratic areas."[50]

One thing most people can agree on, whatever their political beliefs, is that voter rolls are messy, inaccurate, and filled with outdated information. One conservative investigator examining the voter roll overseen by Snipes discovered names of three people who were alive when Grover Cleveland was president in 1890. However, until someone devises a secure and accurate method for cleansing voter rolls, controversies will continue to make headlines. Some believe Congress could fix the problem by implementing more control over the system, but this is unlikely to happen. As the Brennan Center for Justice notes, as long as partisan politics rule the purging process, voter roll maintenance will be "shrouded in secrecy, prone to error, and vulnerable to manipulation."[51]

CHAPTER 5

Criminal Convictions and Voting Rights

In February 2018 members of the Unlock the Vote project were in the Los Angeles County Men's Central Jail. Project volunteers were there to educate inmates about voting rights and register new voters. In California, inmates awaiting trial or in jail for misdemeanors or probation violations are allowed to vote. Californians convicted of a felony cannot vote while in jail or on parole, but their voting rights are automatically restored when they complete their parole. Tim Kornegay, who served over twenty years for receiving stolen property, registered to vote as soon as his sentence was completed. In 2018 Kornegay was among those helping prisoners register at the county jail: "I did my transformation into a better man in [jail], so when I came out I could be ready to serve. Voting for [former inmates] is critically important."[52]

In California, only around three-quarters of 1 percent of the population is prevented from voting due to felony convictions. And as one of the most solidly Democratic states in the country, California has some of the most liberal laws concerning voting rights for lawbreakers. This is especially true when compared to Florida, Iowa, and Kentucky, where felons are barred from voting even after they have served their time and are no longer on parole or probation. This policy is known as felony disenfranchisement. Other states, including Mississippi, Alabama, Arizona, Wyoming, Nevada, and Tennessee, have varying degrees of felony disenfranchisement.

In some states, felons are permanently prohibited from voting after committing serious crimes, including rape, murder, or treason. Other states add crimes to the list that might include assault, financial crimes, and even theft. Some states are far more lenient. In Maine and Vermont, for example, felons never lose their right to vote, even while they are incarcerated.

In 2016 around 2.5 percent of all voting-age Americans, or one in forty adults, were barred from voting due to felony disenfranchisement. During that presidential election year, 6.1 million Americans were prohibited from casting a ballot. More than three-quarters of these disenfranchised citizens—4.7 million people—were not incarcerated. They were living in American communities, working, paying taxes, and raising families. However, they had felony records or had not yet completed the terms of their parole. Supporters of felony disenfranchisement maintain that the punishment fits the crime. As Roger Clegg, the president and general counsel of the conservative think tank the Center for Equal Opportunity, says, "It makes sense that felons should lose their right to vote. You don't have a right to make the laws if you aren't willing to follow them yourself. To participate in self-government, you must be willing to accept the rule of law."[53]

> "It makes sense that felons should lose their right to vote. You don't have a right to make the laws if you aren't willing to follow them yourself."[53]
>
> —Roger Clegg, president and general counsel of the Center for Equal Opportunity

Targeting African Americans

The United States is one of the few modern democracies in the world that prohibits voting because of past criminal convictions. Critics believe it is a sign that America has not kept up with the progressive attitudes of most other nations. Some argue the laws are designed to perpetually punish rather than rehabilitate criminals. Many of these critics are concerned that the laws disproportionately impact people of color. According to the Sentencing

Prisoners play basketball at a Florida correctional facility. More strict than most states, Florida prohibits felons from voting even after they serve their time and are no longer on parole or probation.

Project, a prisoner advocacy organization, one in every thirteen voting-age African Americans is disenfranchised nationally. By comparison, only one in fifty-six nonblack Americans is prohibited from casting a ballot. In some states the disenfranchisement rate for black citizens is even higher. In Kentucky, over 26 percent of black adults are disenfranchised, and in Florida, Tennessee, and Virginia that number is around 21 percent.

Some critics say felony disenfranchisement laws are part of America's racist past. In the decades after the Civil War, states in the South passed dozens of laws aimed at disenfranchising African

Americans who had recently gained the right to vote. Harsh penalties were applied to offenses that whites believed might be commonly committed by African Americans. These crimes included arson, burglary, and assaulting a white woman. In some southern states, it was a felony for a black person to possess a firearm or to make liquor. Furthermore, many crimes that were considered misdemeanors or trivial offenses when committed by whites were treated as felonies when committed by African Americans. Today some commentators contend that disenfranchisement laws are a legacy of the attitudes that tried to keep blacks from participating in the nation's democracy.

A War on Drugs and Voting Rights

The main source of felony disenfranchisement for African Americans in the modern era can be traced to the ongoing war on drugs. Many statisticians have noted that harsh criminal sentences for possessing or selling drugs have been unequally applied to people of color for decades. Studies consistently show that white Americans are just as likely to sell and use drugs, but African Americans are far more likely to go to prison for drug offenses. Quoting figures from a National Research Council report entitled *The Growth of Incarceration in the United States*, black activist Van Jones states, "We wind up getting arrested, not 50 percent more. We wind up going to prison six times more because there seems to be some institutional bias."[54]

When Republican president Richard Nixon began the drug war in 1971, his intentions were clear. Nixon understood that criminalizing drug use would neutralize his political foes who consisted of long-haired Vietnam War protesters and black civil rights activists. As Nixon's chief policy adviser, John Ehrlichman, admitted in 1994,

We knew we couldn't make it illegal to be either against the war or black, but by getting the public to associate the

60

hippies with marijuana and blacks with heroin, and then criminalizing both heavily, we could disrupt those communities. We could arrest their leaders, raid their homes, break up their meetings, and vilify them night after night on the evening news. Did we know we were lying about the drugs? Of course we did.[55]

The war on drugs intensified throughout the 1980s and 1990s. Lawmakers from both political parties passed a series of draconian drug-sentencing laws that took aim at low-level street dealers in communities of color. In some large cities, such as Baltimore, African American men accounted for 80 percent of drug arrests. As a result, the number of people incarcerated in federal prisons for nonviolent felony drug offenses in the United States went from fifty thousand in 1980 to over four hundred thousand in 1997.

By 2000 over half a million African Americans were in state and federal custody largely due to the war on drugs. Although African Americans made up 12 percent of the US population, they

Studies consistently show that while white Americans are just as likely to sell and use drugs, African Americans are far more likely to go to prison for drug offenses.

accounted for 46 percent of the incarcerated population. On average, African American males were almost nine times more likely to be imprisoned than white males.

Denying Clemency in Florida

Felony disenfranchisement in Florida was higher than anywhere else in the United States at the end of the 1990s. The state's prison population had exploded, and at that time 19 percent of voting-age African Americans in the state were disenfranchised

Ex-felons Should Not Be Able to Vote

Roger Clegg is the president and general counsel of the Center for Equal Opportunity, a conservative think tank. Clegg explains why he supports laws that prevent felons from voting:

> We don't let everyone vote—not children, not noncitizens, not the mentally incompetent. There are certain minimum and objective standards of trustworthiness, responsibility, and commitment to our laws that we require before people are entrusted with a role in the solemn enterprise of self-government. Those who have committed serious crimes against their fellow citizens don't meet those standards. . . .
>
> [It is] often asserted that felon disenfranchisement laws are "racist." That's not true. . . . To be sure, they may have a disproportionate impact on some racial groups, because at any point in time there are always going be some groups that statistically commit more crimes than others. . . . [But] the people whose voting rights will be diluted the most if criminals are allowed to vote are the law-abiding people in high-crime areas, who are themselves disproportionately black and Latino. . . . People can be forgiven, but that does not mean there aren't consequences for wrongdoing.

Roger Clegg, "Felons and the Vote," Center for Equal Opportunity, March 30, 2015. www.ceousa.org.

Ex-felons Should Have Voting Rights

Janai S. Nelson is a law professor who acts as council for the Legal Defense and Educational Fund of the National Association for the Advancement of Colored People. In the excerpted editorial below, Nelson argues that felony disenfranchisement laws have a racist past and should be permanently banned.

> Like the antiquated laws that excluded women, people of color and the poor from the ballot box, felon disenfranchisement laws are an anti-democratic tool with a sordid history of discrimination. Today, they intersect with the profound racial disparities in the U.S. criminal justice system to keep one out of every 13 African-Americans from voting. . . . Modern support for felon disenfranchisement is often based on negative assumptions about how someone's identity, status or past behavior will inform his or her choices in the ballot box. . . .

> We should be doing everything possible to successfully integrate the estimated 636,000 people released from prisons each year into society. . . . In a country that has the highest incarceration rate of any modern democratic nation, laws that prevent prisoners from voting also imprison our democracy. The disfranchisement of people with felony convictions is one of the most pressing civil rights issues of our time.

Janai S. Nelson, "Felon Disenfranchisement Is Anti-Democratic," *New York Times*, April 22, 2016. www.nytimes.com.

ex-felons. The high rate of disenfranchised Floridians put the issue on the front pages after the 2000 presidential election between George W. Bush and Al Gore. Election experts noted that five hundred thousand ex-felons in Florida were unable to cast a ballot in a state Bush won by 537 votes.

Bush's victory was even more controversial because his brother, Jeb Bush, was Florida's governor. In Florida, disenfranchised ex-felons can petition the governor to restore their rights to vote, serve on a jury, and run for office. The governor can then choose whether to restore the prisoners' rights, a process called granting clemency. However, according to Florida law, "the Governor has the unfettered discretion to deny clemency at any time, for any reason."[56] And in the run-up to the close election in 2000, Governor Bush used his discretion to deny clemency to four-fifths of the petitioners before him. In 2004 Bush told reporters, "I'm confident in the [clemency] process. I think it's a fair process."[57] However, critics believe denying prisoners voting rights is a partisan issue because Florida is almost evenly divided between Republican and Democratic voters. As political science professor Aubrey Jewett explains, "Many statewide [Florida] elections are quite close. Keeping potentially tens of thousands or hundreds of thousands off the rolls when a majority of those voters are probably going to vote Democratic, you can't help but suspect partisan motivation."[58]

In 2018 over 27 percent of all disenfranchised felons in the United States lived in Florida, and the situation has changed little

The 2000 presidential election between George W. Bush (on left) and Al Gore (on right) highlighted voting issues in Florida. Election experts noted that 500,000 ex-felons were unable to vote in a state that Bush won by a mere 537 votes.

since 2000. Florida's Republican governor, Rick Scott, elected in 2011, had granted clemency to fewer than two thousand ex-felons as of 2018. Scott turned down clemency for over eighteen thousand petitioners. Scott spokesperson John Tupps defended the process: "Officials elected by Floridians, not judges, have the authority to determine Florida's clemency process for convicted felons. This is outlined in Florida's Constitution and has been in place for more than a century and under multiple gubernatorial administrations."[59]

> "Keeping potentially tens of thousands or hundreds of thousands off the rolls when a majority of those voters are probably going to vote Democratic, you can't help but suspect partisan motivation."[58]
>
> —Political science professor Aubrey Jewett

Florida's strict clemency law has generated numerous lawsuits. In 2018 a federal district court judge in Tallahassee struck down the law as unconstitutional. The judge also noted several instances where felons who said they were Republicans were granted clemency while those who stated otherwise were denied clemency. Scott appealed the case, which will likely be heard by the Supreme Court by 2020. While the case winds its way through the court system, the voter advocacy group Floridians for a Fair Democracy launched a campaign called Florida Second Chances. In 2018 the group was collecting signatures for a ballot initiative that would allow Florida voters to amend the state constitution to eliminate felony disenfranchisement. If the ballot initiative passes, Floridians with felony convictions, who have completed their sentences, will have their voting rights automatically restored.

Complex and Confusing

In most states with felony disenfranchisement laws, those who try to restore their voting rights face processes that are inconsistent and confusing. For example, due to loopholes in the law in Tennessee, those who were convicted of a felony between 1973 and 1981 never lost their right to vote. But felons who committed nonviolent crimes after 1982—and finished their sentences—have to apply to the state parole board to restore their voting rights. Ex-felons have to prove they paid all court-imposed fines, financial obligations such as child support, and restitution (court-ordered payments to crime victims). This policy places a burden on low-income lawbreakers, who have a difficult time finding meaningful employment due to their prison records.

In Mississippi, some felons who have completed their sentences and probation can regain their voting rights. However, the state defines twenty-two crimes that permanently disenfranchise residents, including bribery, theft, arson, welfare fraud, perjury, forgery, and embezzlement. The long list of crimes prevented an estimated 218,000 people from voting in Mississippi in 2016. Only around 7 percent of the disenfranchised, or 15,260 citizens, were incarcerated. The rest had completed their sentences or were living in their communities on parole or probation. Overall, 9.6 percent of all adults in Mississippi—nearly one in ten—are disenfranchised due to felony convictions.

In Alabama, an amendment to the 1901 constitution stripped voting rights from anyone committing a crime involving what was called *moral turpitude*. This vague term is defined as an act that gravely violates the accepted moral standards of the community. Judges can add a charge of moral turpitude to misdemeanors, felonies, and even acts not punishable by law. The white supremacists who promoted the law were clear about their motives. During the early 1900s one politician said that the moral turpitude clause was added to the Alabama constitution to "establish white supremacy in this state."[60]

The moral turpitude clause was used to disenfranchise voters in Alabama until 1985, when the Supreme Court unanimously ruled that it was unconstitutional. But in 1996 Alabama lawmakers approved what was called Amendment 579, which reinserted the moral turpitude clause into the state constitution. In the following years, thousands of voters were disenfranchised for crimes involving moral turpitude. However, the state did not have a list or legal code that defined the crime of moral turpitude. When an ex-felon tried to register to vote, each county registrar could determine whether the law applied to the individual's crimes. For example, some county registrars might consider simple marijuana possession to be a crime of moral turpitude, but another might only apply the clause to the sale and distribution of marijuana. Although the law occupied a gray area, the outcome was clear. An astounding 15 percent of qualified black voters in Alabama could not cast a ballot during the 1990s because of felony disenfranchisement. Less than 5 percent of the white population was affected.

In 2017 Alabama governor Kay Ivey signed legislation to clarify that only the most severe felonies constituted moral turpitude. However, officials were not interested in educating the public about the change. In 2018 Danielle Lang, a lawyer at the Campaign Legal Center, a voter advocacy group, sued the state. Lang was hoping to force officials to notify the disenfranchised that they could now register to vote. Lang criticized Alabama officials: "This is confusion that was wrought by the state. Under this newfound definition [of moral turpitude], it turns out [some] do have the right to vote. I don't see how anyone would know that unless they're kind of legislative junkies."[61] Additionally, the law did not specify how disenfranchised citizens would go about regaining their voting rights. Activists say ex-felons might need to hire lawyers to help them restore their voting rights, an additional expense few could afford.

Granting Second Chances

As the situation in Alabama illustrates, voting rights restoration is subject to the whims of legislatures and can change with the political winds. Iowa provides a good example of how partisan politics can affect voting rights. In 2005 Iowa's Democratic governor, Tom Vilsack, issued an executive order that automatically restored voting rights to ex-felons. The order was rescinded by Republican governor Terry Branstad in 2011. In Florida in 2007, Governor Charlie Crist, a political independent, signed an order that automatically restored voting rights to persons with nonviolent felonies.

More than 150,000 had their rights restored. Florida's parole commission conducted a study in 2011 that showed members of this group had a 20 percent lower chance of returning to prison than those who did not have their voting rights restored. The commission concluded that restoring voting rights encouraged greater social stability among nonviolent former inmates. And by lowering rates of recidivism (the tendency of a convicted criminal to reoffend), the state saved tens of millions of dollars. The order was reversed in 2011 by Rick Scott, who instituted a rule that ex-felons would have to wait five years after completing their sentences before applying for clemency. Champions of the 2007 order were stunned by the new policy.

According to polls, 80 percent of Americans believe that citizens who have completed their sentences should be allowed to vote, and 66 percent say even those on parole or probation should have the franchise. As a result, some states have modified their policies. These changes are based on the idea that the voting process should be free and fair to all and that it makes sense to do away with laws that have roots in the nineteenth century. Voting is one of the basic rights granted to citizens of the United States. And many believe in granting second chances to those who have paid their dues for their crimes and have made the commitment to become honest citizens.

Introduction: Voting Rights Restrictions

1. Quoted in Ari Berman, "How the GOP Rigs Elections," *Rolling Stone*, February 8–22, 2018, p. 29.
2. Quoted in Jonathan Blitzer, "Trump and the Truth: The 'Rigged' Election," *New Yorker*, October 8, 2016. www.newyorker.com.
3. Quoted in Berman, "How the GOP Rigs Elections," p. 29.
4. Quoted in Michael Wines, "Some Republicans Acknowledge Leveraging Voter ID Laws for Political Gain," *New York Times*, September 16, 2016. www.nytimes.com.

Chapter 1: The Voting Rights Act

5. Quoted in Charles Marsh, "God's Long Summer," *Washington Post*. www.washingtonpost.com.
6. Quoted in Marsh," God's Long Summer."
7. John Lewis, "The Voting Rights Act: Ensuring Dignity and Democracy," *Human Rights*, Spring 2005, vol. 32, no. 2. www.americanbar.org.
8. Lewis, "The Voting Rights Act."
9. Quoted in Lewis, "The Voting Rights Act."
10. Quoted in Kenneth T. Walsh, "Voting Rights Still a Hot-Button Issue," *U.S. News & World Report*, August 4, 2015. www.usnews.com.
11. Lewis, "The Voting Rights Act."
12. Quoted in Ed Pilkington, "Texas Rushes Ahead with Voter ID Law After Supreme Court Decision," *Guardian* (US edition), June 25, 2013. www.theguardian.com.
13. Quoted in Nina Totenberg, "Supreme Court: Congress Has to Fix Broken Voting Rights Act," *All Things Considered*, NPR, June 25, 2013. www.npr.org.
14. Quoted in Lawrence Hurley, "Supreme Court Guts Key Part of Landmark Voting Rights Act," Reuters, June 25, 2013. www.reuters.com.
15. Quoted in Theodore M. Shaw and Vishal Agraharkar, "Voting Against Discrimination: The Crucial Step America Took 50 Years ago to Affirm Its Democratic Values Is Under Unprecedented Assault," *New York Daily News*, August 2, 2015. www.nydailynews.com.

16. Quoted in Walsh, "Voting Rights Still a Hot-Button Issue."

17. Quoted in Alicia Petska and Tiffany Holland, "Goodlatte: Voting Rights Act Remains Strong Without Amendment," *Roanoke Times*, June 22, 2015. www.roanoke.com.

18. Quoted in Rebecca Beitsch, "New Voter ID Rules, Other Election Changes Could Cause Confusion," *PBS NewsHour*, October 19, 2016. www.pbs.org.

Chapter 2: Voter IDs and Early Voting

19. Quoted in Hans von Spakovsky, "Voter Photo Identification: Protecting the Security of Elections," Heritage Foundation, July 13, 2011. www.heritage.org.

20. Quoted in Topher Sanders, "A Wisconsin Republican Looks Back with Regret at Voter ID and Redistricting Fights," ProPublica, July 2, 2017. www.propublica.org.

21. Quoted in Ari Berman, "A 90-Year-Old Woman Who's Voted Since 1948 Was Disenfranchised by Wisconsin's Voter-ID Law," *Nation*, October 5, 2016. www.thenation.com.

22. Quoted in Andrew Cohen, "A Federal Judge Searches for Voter Fraud in Wisconsin and Finds None," *Atlantic*, April 30, 2014. www.theatlantic.com.

23. Quoted in Monica Davey and Steven Yaccino, "Federal Judge Strikes Down Wisconsin Law Requiring Voter ID at Polls," *New York Times*, April 29, 2014. www.nytimes.com.

24. Ari Berman, "The GOP's Attack on Voting Rights Was the Most Under-covered Story of 2016," *Nation*, November 9, 2016. www.thenation.com.

25. Quoted in Aaron Blake, "North Carolina Governor Signs Extensive Voter ID Law," *Washington Post*, August 12, 2013. www.washingtonpost.com.

26. Quoted in Colin Campbell, "NC Republican Party Seeks 'Party Line Changes' to Limit Early Voting Hours," *Raleigh (NC) News Observer*, August 17, 2016. www.newsobserver.com.

27. William Wan, "Inside the Republican Creation of the North Carolina Voting Bill Dubbed the 'Monster' Law," *Washington Post*, September 2, 2016. www.washingtonpost.com.

28. Quoted in Camila Domonoske, "Supreme Court Declines Republican Bid to Revive North Carolina Voter ID Law," *Two-Way* (blog), NPR, May 15, 2017. www.npr.org.

29. Quoted in Adam Liptak and Michael Wines, "Strict North Carolina Voter ID Law Thwarted After Supreme Court Rejects Case," *New York Times*, May 15, 2017. www.nytimes.com.

30. Quoted in Liptak and Wines, "Strict North Carolina Voter ID Law Thwarted After Supreme Court Rejects Case."

Chapter 3: Polling Place Problems

31. Leslie Feldman, "My Arizona Voting Disaster: Four-Hour Lines, No Ballots, and Overflowing Toilets," *Washington Post*, April 14, 2016. www.washingtonpost.com.
32. Quote in Matt Vasilogambros, "Voting Lines Are Shorter—but Mostly for Whites," *Huffington Post*, February 15, 2018. www.huffingtonpost.com.
33. Quoted in Vasilogambros, "Voting Lines Are Shorter."
34. Quoted in Scott Simpson, "The Great Poll Closure," Leadership Conference Education Fund, 2016. http://civilrights docs.info.
35. Quoted in Elena Mejia Lutz, "Report: Texas Has Closed More Polling Places Since Court Ruling," Texas Tribune, November 4, 2016. www.texastribune.org.
36. Quoted in Lutz, "Report."
37. Simpson, "The Great Poll Closure."
38. Kevin Roose, "A Solution to Hackers? More Hackers," *New York Times*, August 2, 2017. www.nytimes.com.
39. Matt Blaze et al., "DEFCON 25: Voting Machine Hacking Village," DEFCON, September 2017. www.defcon.org.
40. Quoted in Joseph Cox, "The 2016 Election Wasn't Hacked, but the 2020 Election Could Be," *Motherboard*, December 28, 2016. https://motherboard.vice.com.
41. Jonathan Simon, "19 Big Myths About Our Elections That the Government and Media Hope You'll Believe," Code Red, July 2, 2017. http://codered2014.com.

Chapter 4: Purging Voter Rolls

42. Quoted in Derek Hawkins, "Purged from Voting Rolls While Deployed, Ohio Vet Demands Answers," *Washington Post*, January 13, 2018. www.washingtonpost.com.
43. Quoted in Andy Sullivan and Grant Smith, "Use It or Lose It: Occasional Ohio Voters May Be Shut Out in November," Reuters, June 2, 2016. www.reuters.com.
44. Quoted in Sullivan and Smith, "Use It or Lose It."
45. Quoted in Christopher Ingraham, "This Anti-Voter-Fraud Program Gets It Wrong over 99 Percent of the Time. The GOP Wants to Take It Nationwide," *Washington Post*, July 20, 2017. www.washingtonpost.com.

46. Quoted in Desiree Taliaferro, "Kobach Secures Ninth Voter Fraud Conviction," State of Kansas, Office of the Secretary of State, May 3, 2017. www.sos.ks.gov.
47. Quoted in Greg Palast, "The GOP's Stealth War Against Voters," *Rolling Stone*, August 24, 2016. www.rollingstone.com.
48. Quoted in Palast, "The GOP's Stealth War Against Voters."
49. Quoted in Michael Wines, "Culling Voter Rolls: Battling over Who Even Gets to Go to the Polls," *New York Times*, November 25, 2017. www.nytimes.com.
50. Quoted in Wines, "Culling Voter Rolls."
51. Quoted in Jack Dention, "Why Are So Many People Registered to Vote in Multiple States?," *Pacific Standard*, January 27, 2017. https://psmag.com.

Chapter 5: Criminal Convictions and Voting Rights

52. Quoted in Michael Livingston, "Voter Registration Drive Makes Inroads in Unexpected Territory: County Jails," *Los Angeles Times*, February 26, 2018. www.latimes.com.
53. Roger Clegg, "Felons and the Vote," Center for Equal Opportunity, March 30, 2015. www.ceousa.org.
54. Quoted in C. Eugene Emery Jr., "Van Jones Claim on Drug Use, Imprisonment Rates for Blacks, Whites Is Mostly Accurate," PunditFact, July 13, 2016. www.politifact.com.
55. Quoted in German Lopez, "Nixon Official: Real Reason for the Drug War Was to Criminalize Black People and Hippies," Vox, March 23, 2016. www.vox.com.
56. Quoted in Garrett Eps, "The 'Slave Power' Behind Florida's Felon Disenfranchisement," *Atlantic*, February 4, 2018. www.theatlantic.com.
57. Quoted in Tamara Lush, "Felons Take Their Case to the Governor," *St. Petersburg Times*, June 18, 2004. www.sptimes.com.
58. Quoted in Pema Levy, "How Jeb Bush Enlisted in Florida's War on Black Voters," *Mother Jones*, October 27, 2015. www.motherjones.com.
59. Quoted in Gray Rohrer, "Gov. Scott Defends How State Restores Voting Rights of Felons," *Orlando Sentinel*, February 12, 2018. www.orlandosentinel.com.
60. Quoted in Mark Joseph Stern, "Alabama's Failure of Moral Turpitude," *Slate*, October 6, 2016. www.slate.com.
61. Quoted in Sam Levine, "Alabama Won't Help Disenfranchised Citizens Understand If They Can Now Vote," *Huffington Post*, June 21, 2017. www.huffingtonpost.com.

American Civil Liberties Union (ACLU)

125 Broad St.
New York, NY 10004
www.aclu.org

The ACLU defends the rights and liberties guaranteed by the US Constitution. Lawsuits filed by the organization have been instrumental in ending discriminatory laws and policies designed to limit voting rights.

Brennan Center for Justice

120 Broadway
New York, NY 10271
www.brennancenter.org

The Brennan Center for Justice is a nonpartisan organization dedicated to democracy and equal justice. The center is one of the leading institutions defending voting rights and fighting efforts to purge voter rolls, shut down polling places, and disenfranchise minority voters.

League of Women Voters

1730 M St. NW
Washington, DC 20036
www.lwv.org

The League of Women Voters is a nonpartisan organization committed to helping women gain a larger role in political affairs. The league lobbies against voter ID laws, works to make voter registration easier, and supports efforts to extend the franchise to ex-felons and others shut out of the voting process.

Legal Defense and Educational Fund

National Association for the Advancement of Colored People (NAACP)
40 Rector St.
New York, NY 10006
www.naacpldf.org

The Legal Defense and Educational Fund is the legal arm of the NAACP civil rights organization, which fights for racial justice through litigation, advocacy, and public education. The fund focuses on criminal justice reform, economic equality, and ending restrictions on voting rights.

Public Interest Legal Foundation (PILF)

32 E. Washington St.
Indianapolis, IN 46204
https://publicinterestlegal.org

PILF is a conservative organization that works to fight fraud in American elections by ensuring voter rolls are cleansed of double voters and deceased citizens. The foundation files lawsuits against election officials to force them to disclose alleged noncitizen voter records.

Sentencing Project

1705 DeSales St. NW
Washington, DC 20036
www.sentencingproject.org

The Sentencing Project was founded in 1986 to ensure a fair and effective criminal justice system. The project conducts studies, formulates policies, and files lawsuits to end felony disenfranchisement and fight racial disparities in the courts.

True the Vote

https://truethevote.org

True the Vote is a conservative vote-monitoring organization dedicated to stopping voter fraud by promoting voter ID laws and training members to monitor polling places on election day.

FOR FURTHER RESEARCH

Books

Jeff Fleischer, *Votes of Confidence: A Young Person's Guide to American Elections*. San Francisco: Zest, 2018.

Liz Idzikowski, *The Electoral College and the Popular Vote*. New York: Greenhaven, 2018.

Zachary Michael Jack, *March of the Suffragettes: Rosalie Gardiner Jones and the March for Voting Rights*. San Francisco: Zest, 2017.

John Lewis, *March*. Marietta, GA: Top Shelf, 2016.

Lynda Blackmon Lowery, *Turning 15 on the Road to Freedom: My Story of the 1965 Selma Voting Rights March*. New York: Penguin, 2016.

Daniel McCool, *The Most Fundamental Right: Contrasting Perspectives on the Voting Rights Act*. Bloomington: Indiana University Press, 2012.

Internet Sources

Aaron Blake, "North Carolina Governor Signs Extensive Voter ID Law," *Washington Post*, August 12, 2013. www .washingtonpost.com/news/post-politics/wp/2013/08/12 /north-carolina-governor-signs-extensive-voter-id-law/?utm _term=.c47851b579fb.

Matt Blaze et al., "DEFCON 25: Voting Machine Hacking Village," DEFCON, September 2017. www.defcon.org/images /defcon-25/DEF%20CON%2025%20voting%20village%20 report.pdf.

Jessica Huseman and Derek Willis, "The Voter Fraud Commission Wants Your Data—but Experts Say They Can't Keep It Safe," ProPublica, October 23, 2017. www.propublica .org/article/crosscheck-the-voter-fraud-commission-wants -your-data-keep-it-safe.

Charles Marsh, "God's Long Summer," *Washington Post*. www.washingtonpost.com/wp-srv/style/longterm/books /chap1/godslongsummer.htm.

Jonathan Simon, "19 Big Myths About Our Elections That the Government and Media Hope You'll Believe," Code Red, July 2, 2017. http://codered2014.com/19-big-myths-elections-government-media-dont-want-know.

Scott Simpson, "The Great Poll Closure," Leadership Conference Education Fund, 2016. http://civilrightsdocs.info/pdf/reports/2016/poll-closure-report-web.pdf.

Jason Snead, "Voter Fraud Is Real. This Searchable Database Proves It," Heritage Foundation, November 1, 2017. www.heritage.org/election-integrity/commentary/voter-fraud-real-searchable-database-proves-it.

Hans von Spakovsky, "Voter Photo Identification: Protecting the Security of Elections," Heritage Foundation, July 13, 2011. www.heritage.org/report/voter-photo-identification-protecting-the-security-elections.

William Wan, "Inside the Republican Creation of the North Carolina Voting Bill Dubbed the 'Monster' Law," *Washington Post*, September 2, 2016. www.washingtonpost.com/politics/courts_law/inside-the-republican-creation-of-the-north-carolina-voting-bill-dubbed-the-monster-law/2016/09/01/79162398-6adf-11e6-8225-fbb8a6fc65bc_story.html?utm_term=.6ceb412b82a6.

Michael Wines, "Some Republicans Acknowledge Leveraging Voter ID Laws for Political Gain," *New York Times*, September 16, 2016. www.nytimes.com/2016/09/17/us/some-republicans-acknowledge-leveraging-voter-id-laws-for-political-gain.html.

INDEX

PICTURE CREDITS

Cover: Charles Mann/iStockphoto.com

7: YinYang/iStockphoto.com

11: Associated Press

14: Associated Press

19: Mike Theiler/Reuters/Newscom

24: Lisa F. Young/Shutterstock.com

27: thad/iStockphoto.com

30: Christian Gooden/TNS/Newscom

37: Bill Dowling/Shutterstock.com

40: Associated Press

43: Bing Wen/iStockphoto.com

49: Rena Schild/iStockphoto.com

53: Sipa USA/TNS/Newscom

55: Burlingham/Shutterstock.com

59: Joseph Sohm/Shutterstock.com

61: Syda Productions/Shutterstock.com

64: Pete Souza/KRT/Newscom